UNSHAKEN LEADERSHIP

A Practical Blueprint for Overcoming Challenges, Learning from Mistakes, and Growing in Confidence.

KEYIMANI L. ALFORD

This is a work of nonfiction. All of the reported incidents occurred as recorded here, to the best of my recollection and records. The names have been changed in order to protect character identities. Any resulting resemblance to persons living or dead is entirely coincidental and unintentional. No part of this book may be used or reproduced in any manner without prior written permission except in the case of brief quotations embodied in critical articles or reviews.

At the time of this publication, the URLs displayed in this book refer to existing websites on the Internet. Keywords Unlocked, LLC is not responsible for, and should not be deemed to endorse or recommend any website other than its own or any content available on the Internet not created by Keywords Unlocked, LLC.

Copyright © 2025 by Keyimani L. Alford
All rights reserved.

Published and printed in the United States of America
by Keywords Unlocked, LLC.

eBook ISBN: 979-8-9920869-3-5
Paperback ISBN: 979-8-9920869-4-2
Hardcover ISBN: 979-8-9920869-5-9

For More Information Contact:
Keywords Unlocked, LLC.
6969 N. Port Washington Road, Suite B150, #1025
Glendale, Wisconsin 53217
www.drkeyspeaks.com

10 9 8 7 6 5 4 3 2 1

By
Keyimani L. Alford

Unshaken Leadership: A Blueprint for Overcoming Challenges, Learning from Mistakes, and Growing in Confidence

Oakland Hills, Milwaukee Rivers

Oakland Hills, Milwaukee Rivers Workbook: A Guide for Faith and Biblical Application

Keywords Unlocked: 2025-2026 Ultimate Motivational Monthly Planner: A Guide to Accomplishing Your Goals

To every aspiring leader seeking insight
before stepping into leadership,
I applaud you.

To every new leader who understands that reaching
your full potential comes from learning from others,
I celebrate you.

To every experienced leader who understands
there is always more to learn,
I admire you.

May this book be your guide.

When you learn, teach. When you get, give.
— *Maya Angelou*

Contents

A Note from Dr. Key   1

PART ONE:
LIVING YOUR TRUTH

Introduction   9

CHAPTER ONE
Unlocking Leadership Potential   17

CHAPTER TWO
Two Truths: Idea and Reality   24

CHAPTER THREE
Building Confidence in Risks   29

CHAPTER FOUR
The Watchful Eyes   39

PART TWO:
PURPOSEFUL LEADERSHIP ADVICE

CHAPTER FIVE
Navigating the Critics   49

CHAPTER SIX
The Collaborative North Star   61

CHAPTER SEVEN
Inauthentic Leadership   77

PART THREE: PRIORITIZING THE MATTERS

CHAPTER EIGHT
TBD   87

CHAPTER NINE
A Balancing Act   98

CHAPTER TEN
Taking Ownership of YOU   110

PART FOUR: RELATIONSHIP BUILDING

CHAPTER ELEVEN
Changing Leadership Colors   127

CHAPTER TWELVE
The Power of Words   137

CHAPTER THIRTEEN
Your Choice: Respond or React   143

CHAPTER FOURTEEN
Intentional Leadership   149

PART FIVE: THE UNSHAKEN LEADER

Conclusion   159

End Notes   163

Acknowledgments   167

About the Author   169

UNSHAKEN LEADERSHIP

un•shak•en:
not disturbed from a firm position or state; steadfast and unwavering
lead•er•ship:
the action of leading a group of people or an organization

A Note from Dr. Key

For once in my life, I'm being selfish, and I'll tell you why. Writing these pages wasn't just about sharing theories or frameworks; it was about giving you, the reader, something raw and real—the truth about leadership as I've lived it. The late nights, the tough calls, the moments of doubt, and the hard-earned lessons that no one warns you about. This isn't a polished highlight reel; it's the unfiltered reality of what it takes to lead with impact.

So, if you're looking for sugar-coated advice, this might not be the book for you. But if you're ready for honest insights, personal stories, and the kind of leadership lessons that come from experience—not just textbooks—then let's dive in.

I wrote this book for those stepping into their first management role, those who have been in the trenches for years, and those still trying to figure out what leadership really means. There was one reality people don't warn you about: **making mistakes.** Yet, we all do! We often walk into management roles believing we're supposed to have all the answers, solve every problem, and never stumble. **I have to warn you now: leadership is much messier than that.** And, this book is to help you navigate it.

Now, don't get me wrong—leading people, driving a mission, and implementing bold strategies are rewarding. But leadership also comes with its fair share of challenges, growing pains, and *"What the hell did I just get myself into?"* moments. I won't lie or let you think otherwise.

So, what's my intention here? To share these lessons with you—from my life to yours—as a lifeline. Will you take heed? Who knows. But we'll share them with you all the same.

In my two decades of leading teams across different industries—higher education, business, fast food, nonprofits, and even the church— I have made mistakes—some minor, some significant, and a few downright embarrassing. But every single one of them taught me something invaluable—not just about leadership, but about myself.

I want to help you solve future problems by avoiding pitfalls and equipping you with the tools and perspectives I wish I had at the start.

In this book, the vulnerability I share was intentional and necessary. I didn't want to overwhelm you with abstract theories or complicated models. Instead, I wanted to offer practical, real-life lessons. After all, leadership isn't something you perfect by reading a book—it's something you grow into.

But here's my first piece of advice: don't just read this book. **Apply it.** Too many leaders absorb knowledge but never implement it. Don't be that person.

In this book, I will be your leadership companion—your mentor in writing. I'll share the good, the bad, and the downright chaotic moments of my career—not to boast, but to show you that even experienced leaders stumble. More importantly, I'll show you how to recover and grow stronger from those stumbles. The good part.

One of my proudest moments wasn't receiving a title or hitting a milestone—it was hearing a former team member say, **"You inspired me."** That's what leadership is truly about. Not just managing people, **but empowering them to realize their potential.**

My earnest desire is that by the end of this book, you'll feel that same inspiration, motivation, and be better equipped to navigate your personal leadership journey.

This isn't just a collection of anecdotes; it's a mentor in written form, guiding you through the highs and lows of leadership.

Leadership is a balancing act: you have to navigate personalities, emotions, ambitions, and sometimes hidden agendas. You have to make tough decisions—often with incomplete information—and take risks based on your values. Some choices will make you popular. Others? Not so much. That's the weight of leadership. **It requires courage, resilience, and a whole lot of emotional intelligence.**

And let's talk about stress. **According to a study by the American Psychological Association, 77% of people report experiencing work-related stress at some point in their career.**[1] Leadership amplifies that. But stress isn't a reason to run—it's a reason to equip yourself with the right mindset, tools, and support system. That's where this book comes in. **Think of it as part of your leadership survival kit.** It's not an exhaustive guide to every leadership challenge you'll face, but it's a starting point—a source of encouragement, practical strategies, and lessons learned the hard way.

You might be an aspiring leader, eager to step into a role where you can make a difference. Or perhaps you're a new leader, someone a mentor or supervisor saw potential in and entrusted with a team. Or maybe you're an experienced leader, well-versed in the demands of the role but still hungry to grow and improve. Wherever you are on your journey, I applaud you for taking this step.

Now, you might be wondering: **Why should I even listen to this guy?** Fair question.

There are plenty of "well-known" experts who will sell you their **"Five Steps to Becoming an Influential Leader."** But leadership isn't a checklist—it's a journey. **And I'm offering you the lived experiences, the candid moments, and the raw truth** most leadership books gloss over. I've led teams with million-dollar budgets and teams with barely enough resources to function. I've had moments where I felt unstoppable and moments where I cried, wondering if I was cut out for this. Leadership is **not** about having all the answers—it's about figuring things out along the way.

I've stripped away the façade of perfection that often surrounds leadership. This is personal to me and now personal to you. So, here's my challenge to you: **embrace your mistakes.** Don't let them define you—let them refine you. Growth comes from reflection, adaptation, and the courage to keep going. **The best leaders aren't perfect. They're intentional.**

I want you to imagine this—**a quiet evening, ten years from now.** The world outside has settled, the hum of the day giving way to a stillness that invites reflection. You're sitting at your desk, the same one where you've made countless decisions, drafted bold strategies, and wrestled with the weight of leadership. The glow of a single lamp casts long shadows across the room, its soft light illuminating the pages of an open journal where you've been jotting down thoughts—lessons learned, battles fought, and victories, both small and monumental.

As you lean back in your chair, you exhale deeply, letting the years roll back in your mind. **The moments flash before you—the trials that tested you, the setbacks that almost broke you, the decisions that kept you awake at night.** The conversations that challenged you, the choices that defined you, and the moments when you wondered if you had what it took. You remember the first time you had to stand firm when it would have been easier to fold. The moment you learned that failure wasn't the end, but a beginning. The day you finally saw the impact of your leadership, not in numbers or accolades, but in the confidence and growth of those you led.

Your eyes drift toward the bookshelf in the corner of the room. It holds the books that shaped you—the ones that left a mark, the ones you turned to when you needed guidance. And there it is. **A familiar title catches your eye:** *Unshaken Leadership: A Practical Blueprint for Overcoming Challenges, Learning from Mistakes, and Growing in Confidence.*

You reach for it, feeling the weight of its pages, but more than that, the weight of what it represents. **This book wasn't just something you read—it was something you lived.** It met you at a time when you needed clarity. It reminded you of lessons you had tucked away in the back of your mind, waiting for the right moment to be used. It didn't give you all the answers, but it helped you ask the right questions. It challenged you, encouraged you, and in some ways, shaped the leader you became.

Now, you find yourself thinking about the next generation of leaders—the ones standing where you once stood, facing their own uncertainties, wondering if they have what it takes. And you realize something. **You're no longer just the one seeking wisdom—you're the one sharing it.**

This is that moment. **Right now.** The moment **when** you decide that growth isn't just something that happens—it's something you commit to. The moment **when** you recognize that the investment you make in yourself today will become the foundation of the leader you are ten years from now.

And more importantly, this is the moment when you realize that leaders like you don't just endure challenges—you transform them into stepping stones for something greater. You will do amazing things. **And when the time comes, you'll be the one reaching back to help someone else do the same.**

So, congratulations on taking this step to invest in your leadership journey. **Buckle up—this will be an eye-opening ride.** Along the way, you'll discover practical strategies, relatable stories, and insights designed to challenge and inspire you. **I'm honored to be part of your journey—thank you for trusting me,**

Now, **turn the page.** Let's get to work.

PART ONE: LIVING YOUR TRUTH

A mistake doesn't become positive until you learn from it.

Introduction

> "If you think you're leading and no one is following,
> you're just taking a walk."
> **- John C. Maxwell**

Leadership is a multifaceted and, let's be honest, sometimes chaotic phenomenon. Each day, we wake up, put on our professional armor, and march into the office, ready to embrace our teams, tackle challenges, and somehow balance an ever-growing list of responsibilities—both professionally and personally.

At work, we might be the boss, director, executive, or team lead. At home, we're parents, partners, caregivers, or unofficial household problem-solvers. One moment, you're making high-level strategic decisions, and the next, you're negotiating with a toddler over why chicken nuggets don't count as a food group. Regardless of the setting, leadership comes with a set of expectations—ones that are observed and judged, welcomed but not always celebrated, and accepted yet often resisted.

Before stepping into leadership, many of us had this grand idea that leading was about telling people what to do. Admit it, at some point, you envisioned walking into a room, commanding attention, and delegating tasks with the precision of a well-oiled machine. But reality has a funny way of humbling us. The thrill of barking orders might seem appealing, but the true essence of leadership lies in building relationships, cultivating trust, and inspiring others to achieve a shared vision.

The real question is, how do you develop the confidence to make the right decisions, navigate setbacks, and push forward when the weight of leadership feels overwhelming? That's where Unshaken Leadership comes in.

un•shak•en: not disturbed from a firm position or state; steadfast and unwavering.

lead•er•ship: the action of leading a group of people or an organization.

The biggest reality check in leadership? It takes time and energy to figure out what works and what doesn't. The problem is, we no longer have the luxury of waiting 20 to 30 years to master leadership through trial and error. Organizations demand results now, and managers need practical strategies at their fingertips to make an impact.

Unfortunately, many new (and even seasoned) leaders experience a gut-punching realization: sometimes, you think you're leading, but no one is actually following. And that's when you discover that leadership isn't about titles or authority—it's about influence and impact. As one famous quote warns, "If you think you're leading and no one is following, you're just taking a walk." Leadership starts with authenticity, and authenticity builds influence.

For years, I've had the privilege of working in dynamic industries, reading some of the best leadership books, and picking the brains of extraordinary leaders. But through it all, I noticed something troubling: many aspiring leaders and even those already in leadership roles aren't privy to the insights that make the biggest difference.

It took me years of trial and error—some impressive wins, a few embarrassing mistakes, and more "What did I just get myself into?" moments than I'd like to admit—to figure out the strategies that actually work.

One thing that continues to surprise me? Most leadership development programs are missing two critical elements: relatability and applicability. Organizations invest heavily in management training, yet too often, these programs focus on theories rather than real-world execution. Leadership isn't just something you learn—it's something you live, adapt to, and practice daily.

Let me paint a picture for you. Imagine a leadership seminar where you spend eight hours listening to someone talk about "leveraging synergy for cross-functional alignment." Sounds impressive, right? But when Monday morning rolls around, and your team is looking at you for answers, that synergy talk won't save you. What you really need is a practical, real-world approach to handling challenges, making decisions, and leading with confidence.

That's exactly why this book exists.

Unveiling Leadership Insights

We're going to navigate leadership together—not with sugar-coated clichés, but with honest insights, practical strategies, and real-life lessons from those who've been in the trenches.

When writing this book, I surrounded myself with my phone, a dry-erase board, stacks of paper, and one big question: **"What do I wish I had known before stepping into leadership?"** From there, the chapters began to take shape, each one built around the lessons I had learned—sometimes the hard way.

Wanting to ensure I wasn't just relying on my own experiences, I turned to social media and tapped into the collective wisdom of seasoned professionals across various industries. To my surprise, **90% of the topics I had outlined were echoed by others**—leaders from business, education, nonprofits, church administration, and entrepreneurship. That confirmed it: the challenges of leadership are universal, and the lessons in this book will be valuable no matter where or how you lead.

Insight 1: Understanding Your Foundation

Have you ever wondered why you are the way you are? The habits you've formed, the mannerisms you display, or even how you navigate different spaces? It all likely traces back to your lived experiences, especially in workplace cultures. We explore this influence to help leaders better understand their "why" in leading.

Insight 2: Dealing with Idea and Reality.

Ever walked into a leadership role thinking, I've got a plan, and it's brilliant—only to realize that your grand vision collides headfirst with budget cuts, resistant teams, and the ever-dreaded phrase, "That's not how we do things here"? Learning to bridge the gap between vision and execution is one of the first lessons of leadership, and this book will help you do just that.

Insight 3: Taking Risks for Impact.

Taking risks as a leader can feel like jumping off a diving board without knowing if there's water in the pool. And let's be honest—sometimes you miscalculate and belly flop. Mistakes happen. But confidence doesn't come from never failing; it comes from learning how to own your missteps, recover quickly, and move forward with even more insight.

Insight 4: Regulating Opinions of You.

Newsflash: not everyone will agree with you. In fact, Some people will critique your leadership simply because they need something to talk about at lunch. Whether it's handling feedback, addressing doubters, or deciding which opinions actually matter, we're going to unpack the fine art of tuning out the noise while still staying receptive to meaningful input.

Insight 5: Navigating Organizational Politics.

Ah, office politics—the unscheduled game of chess you didn't realize you were playing. Knowing how to manage power dynamics, advocate for your team, and make strategic decisions without losing your sanity is crucial. We'll cover how to play the game without losing yourself in it.

Insight 6: Building a Collaborative Vision.

Ever tried leading a group project where half the team is disengaged, one person thinks they should be in charge, and another just wants to coast? That's leadership in a nutshell. A vision isn't something you declare; it has to be built with your team, not for them. We'll discuss how to craft a vision that actually brings people together rather than pushing them away.

Insight 7: Making Tough Decisions.

This isn't an episode of *Let's Make a Deal*. If leadership were easy, everyone would do it. But making decisions—especially the tough ones—can feel like trying to choose the best option in a no-win scenario. We'll talk about strategies to make confident, values-driven decisions while avoiding analysis paralysis.

Insight 8: Manage Work-Life Balance.

You've got deadlines, a full inbox, a team that needs direction, and somehow, you're also supposed to eat healthy, exercise, and maintain relationships? Right. We'll dive into realistic ways to manage the ever-elusive work-life balance before burnout sneaks up on you.

Insight 9: Self-Development and Improvement.

The best leaders aren't just focused on what they're leading—they're committed to who they are becoming. Leadership isn't just about guiding others; it's about continuously learning, evolving, and improving yourself. We'll explore strategies to keep you growing, adapting, and leading with purpose while addressing stagnation. The enemy of growth.

Insight 10: Altering Leadership Styles.

What worked with one team might fail miserably with another. Leadership isn't about sticking to a single style; it's about adapting while staying true to your core principles. We'll explore how to pivot when needed—without losing credibility or effectiveness.

Insight 11: Speaking Positively.

The way you communicate can either build trust or break it. Whether it's motivating your team, handling difficult conversations, or simply knowing when to shut up and listen, we'll cover how to use your words to inspire, not intimidate.

Insight 12: Emotional Intelligence.

Your technical skills might get you the job, but your emotional intelligence determines how well you lead. From self-awareness to handling conflict, we'll break down why EQ is the secret weapon of every great leader.

Insight 13: Leading with Intention.

Leadership isn't about keeping up appearances; it's about showing up with clarity, purpose, and a deep commitment to making an impact. The strongest leaders don't just react to situations; they lead with intention, vision, and integrity.

Many of us can look at this list and recognize just how valuable these insights would be. It is an extensive collection, but within it lie hidden gems that can shape the way you think, approach challenges, and achieve success in leadership.

Each day, managers make decisions that shape teams, organizations, and communities. They are expected to provide direction, stability, and vision while navigating uncertainty and inspiring confidence. The pressure is immense, yet the most effective leaders embrace challenges, adapt to change, and lead with conviction, remaining steady even when setbacks arise.

No leader has all the answers. Success comes from a willingness to learn, grow, and refine how challenges are approached. Leadership requires recognizing the difference between ideas and reality, taking calculated risks, and recovering from mistakes with resilience. It demands managing scrutiny, navigating workplace politics, and communicating effectively under pressure.

An *unshaken leader* stands firm in adversity, leads with intention, and adapts to meet the needs of those they serve. Strong leadership balances authority and influence, decisiveness and collaboration, driving results and developing people. This kind of leadership is built through experience, self-awareness, and a commitment to growth.

This book is not about theories that sound good but fail in practice. It is about real-world leadership that requires resilience, authenticity, and emotional intelligence. Each chapter provides the tools to navigate challenges with confidence, clarity, and purpose.

Many good things awaits us. Let's unpack these insights!

CHAPTER ONE
Unlocking Leadership Potential

*"Every journey begins with a single step. It is this step
that sets us on the path to the unknown,
a destination prepared for us in life.
Without it, life cannot manifest its true purpose."*

We often hear the rhetorical question, 'Are leaders born or made?' This question invites subjective answers because what truly defines a leader? Does leadership require managing people, or can one lead without an authoritative role? I believe it rests in a simple answer: being willing and able to lead.

Leadership is a skill that can begin to develop at any age, and its foundations are often laid long before formal titles or positions are granted. I know that was the case for me and I'm sure many of you may feel the same way. We often find ourselves in situations or positions where our innate leadership abilities are drawn out of us. Either you aspired to leadership, or someone pulled you into it. They saw something special that you possessed and somehow you found yourself in a position of power. On the other hand, that power comes with a price.

For instance, a young child who organizes a neighborhood game of basketball learns the value of coordination and teamwork. A teenager who takes charge of a school project gains experience in delegation and conflict resolution. These early moments, though informal, plant the seeds of leadership by fostering the ability to inspire, guide, and unite others toward a shared goal. While preparing to write this book I was curious about how many books we have in the world on leadership, and it was eye-opening to discover that there are over 57,000 that exist on Amazon alone, and more are being written each day. Considering that, it's striking how often we fail to acquire the insights necessary to be effective at the onset of our leadership journeys. This book aims to bridge that gap by guiding you from an informational mindset to a transformational one.

For many years I have served in various leadership roles, but my journey began when I was just 14 years old. At the time, no one shared with me the keys to achieving success or how to navigate the inevitable pitfalls of leadership—until now. Along the way, I've identified key elements that can fundamentally transform the way we think and lead if we're exposed to them and integrate them into our personal leadership strategies.

Humble Beginnings of Leadership

My first leadership role was in my local church. I was responsible for the choir, leading adults who were old enough to be my parents. This experience required me to cultivate confidence, articulate a shared vision, and model behaviors that inspired trust and collaboration. It was about singing - yes, but also about creating an environment where everyone felt their contributions were valued and aligned with a common purpose. A very hard position when there isn't a monetary carrot associated with outcomes – a very different perspective when it's our day-to-day jobs where productivity is garnered by earning a living wage. That early opportunity of leading the choir taught me a critical lesson: leadership isn't about age or status. It's about the ability to unite people around a shared goal and empower them to achieve it. This was my first introduction to motivating people and learning how sometimes charismatic leaders drive change in organizations.

My church, located in the inner city of Milwaukee, Wisconsin, presented its own set of challenges as people often found themselves with different needs and priorities. Leading as a 14-year-old was a task. A significant one. Churches, in many instances, are the cornerstone of the community, bustling with vibrant traditions and serving as both a spiritual and cultural hub. In this setting, leadership demanded not only musical talent but also the ability to navigate the nuanced social dynamics of a close-knit congregation where respect was earned, not given, especially by someone so young. The choir I led was a mix of voices, ranging in age from 10 to 50, each bringing their personalities, experiences, and sometimes, egos. Some choir members had strong opinions about how things should be done, and others struggled to respect leadership from someone so young. Sound familiar? I often faced subtle comments or skeptical glances that hinted at a superiority complex among a few older members.

Imagine stepping into the pulpit – the stage or platform – of a lively church where gospel music set the tone for worship, the energy of the congregation filled every pew, and the choir—decked in matching robes or uniforms—held the responsibility of lifting spirits and drawing people closer to faith. It was an environment rich with tradition and passion but also layered with expectations. Balancing these dynamics as a young leader required me to master the art of diplomacy and develop an acute sense of emotional intelligence – a term I didn't know about then but learned later in life.

Lessons in Trust and Conflict Resolution

Quickly I learned that navigating this space meant listening more than speaking. I had to approach disagreements with humility, offering validation to differing perspectives while still steering the group toward a cohesive sound. A sound that sometimes sounded like herding cats and howling dogs, but we worked together to nurture and accomplish the vision that was embedded in my heart. Earning trust wasn't automatic as it required consistency, patience, and an unwavering commitment to the shared goal of excellence. For example, during one particularly challenging rehearsal, a senior choir member openly questioned my direction, suggesting their years of experience outweighed my perspective. Instead of reacting defensively, I acknowledged their experience, listened to their concerns, and proposed a solution that incorporated their feedback while maintaining the choir's focus. Moments like these reinforced the importance of empathy and collaboration in building trust. I leaned heavily on preparation, ensuring I knew the music inside out, to validate my leadership but also maintain my confidence to lead rehearsals with clarity and purpose. When tensions arose, I chose to address them directly but respectfully, understanding that the way I handled conflict would set the tone for the choir.

This experience shaped my character profoundly. It taught me resilience, empathy, and the importance of meeting people where they are. A concept I call the "Chameleon Concept of Leadership" that I discuss later on in this book. It also instilled in me a belief that leadership is not about asserting dominance but about building relationships and fostering collaboration. These lessons would later prove invaluable as I moved into other leadership roles, from the fast-food industry to higher education.

Leadership Evolution: From Choir Stands to Boardrooms

As I grew, my leadership journey expanded into new arenas. In the fast-food industry, I learned the intricacies of operational leadership—managing everything from inventory and staffing to performance evaluations and customer satisfaction. These roles emphasized the importance of accountability and decision-making, as every choice directly affected others. Later in higher education, I discovered the profound weight of leadership, where decisions impacted not just employees but their families and communities as well. I learned that good intentions alone were not enough. Leadership requires intentionality, self-awareness, and a deep understanding of how one's actions ripple outward.

One of the most challenging periods of my career was leading during the global pandemic. The experience reshaped leadership as I once knew it, creating lasting changes that continue to affect industries and individuals. Now in organizations, people increasingly demand better work-life balance, hybrid schedules, remote work options, and greater recognition for their contributions. Observing these shifts, it's clear that more individuals are willing to leave organizations with unsupportive cultures, often without hesitation or notice. These changes remind us that as people and industries evolve, so must we as leaders. I sometimes hear the phrase, "People don't leave jobs, they leave bad managers." While sometimes this is true, this is not always the reality. There are instances where people just aren't in the right job that connects them to their passion and no matter how wonderful their manager is, the job in itself doesn't give them the satisfaction that they long for. I applaud those who seek to align their passion with the work that they provide – it's one of the avenues that allow us to make a genuine impact.

A Harsh Reality of Leadership

I believe leadership or leading is a profound responsibility—a gift to some and a burden to others. It can be a gift because it allows individuals to inspire, guide, and witness the growth of those they lead, creating a lasting impact on their lives and communities. For those who embrace it, leadership offers a unique opportunity to channel their vision, values, and skills into meaningful change. That said, it can also feel like a burden, as the weight of decisions, the expectations of others, and the constant need for adaptability can be overwhelming. Balancing these dualities requires resilience, self-awareness, and an unwavering commitment to the responsibilities at hand. It demands a refined skill set and a strategic mindset to navigate its highs and lows. Yet, it is deeply rewarding to see the fruits of your labor materialize. It is that moment to reflect and say to yourself, "I did that" or better yet, "We did that!"

The Beginning of the Leadership Playbook

Imagine having a "playbook" for this journey—a collection of lessons from those who have walked the path before you. It could be a useful tool that ultimately could prevent you from making some significant mistakes along the way. However, leadership in all its glory, still requires humility, dedication, and a commitment to continual growth. It's not about power, but about relationships and a host of other things.

As you meander through this book, one of the most important lessons I've learned that I want to share with you is, that there is no magical blueprint for success. Regardless of what I share with you, there is still the potential for you to get it wrong. The solitude is that if we take responsibility for our decisions – own it, as I call it – we will experience growth. Every leader is different, and every team presents unique challenges. Nonetheless, some universal truths and lessons can resonate with all of us. By sharing these lessons, I aim to help others navigate common mistakes—learn from them with humility when they occur—and, most importantly, recognize and embrace the boundless potential within themselves. We don't become amazing leaders overnight and you shouldn't take on that expectation. Leadership alone can feel daunting, especially at the start, but the challenges become manageable when we openly share our experiences and learn from one another.

> Leadership begins when you take initiative, guide others toward a shared vision, and cultivate an environment where everyone feels empowered to contribute their best.

Whether you're leading a choir, a team of employees, or an entire organization, the principles remain the same: inspire trust, model excellence, and recognize the profound impact your leadership has on others. This book is a raw and transparent reflection, drawn from years of experiences, challenges, and moments of vulnerability. I hope that the stories and insights shared here will not only help you grow as a leader but also enrich the experiences of those you are privileged to lead.

CHAPTER TWO
Two Truths: Idea and Reality

> *"Often what appears to be true is a myth limiting our progress along the journey."*

Leadership is often viewed through a lens of perfection—a belief that with the right mindset and innate abilities, everything will align seamlessly. Anyone who has spent time in a leadership role knows that reality often paints a very different picture. Leading isn't about achieving flawless execution; it's about navigating complexities, balancing aspirations with tangible limitations, and making decisions that impact people, projects, and organizational goals.

When I first stepped into a leadership role, I carried an idealistic vision. I thought my ideas alone would spark change, motivate teams, and produce results. It wasn't long before I learned that leadership is far more intricate. People have individual needs, departments have competing priorities, and organizations face resource constraints that often clash with even the most well-intentioned plans. For example, you might envision increasing enrollment by 15%, only to realize you lack the staffing or budget to execute the necessary recruitment strategies. Or you might design a student success program to address inequities, only to find the institution's values aren't fully aligned with supporting the most vulnerable populations. These realities are not defeats; they are opportunities to refine your approach and grow as a leader.

The Challenges of Reconciling Ideas and Reality

One of the greatest challenges leaders face is reconciling the gap between ideas and reality. As leaders, we're often encouraged to dream big, and rightfully so, because those ideas are the fuel that drives innovation and progress. But transforming those ideas into actionable plans requires patience, adaptability, and the willingness to face obstacles head-on. It's easy to feel disheartened when your aspirations collide with budget cuts, cultural resistance, or shifting priorities. Yet, it's in these moments that true leadership emerges.

Timing is Everything

I've learned the importance of timing. Not every great idea is ready to flourish immediately. Sometimes, it's a matter of waiting for the right cultural or organizational climate. I recall pitching a professional development initiative to hire graduate students in higher education programs to work in our office for "hands-on" experience. It was ambitious and designed to help aspiring professionals gain credentials and advance their careers while meeting their program requirements. But, the timing couldn't have been worse. The organization was grappling with financial challenges, and the opportunity was seen as a luxury rather than a necessity. While disappointing, I took the feedback to heart, refined the proposal, and reintroduced it a few years later when conditions had improved. This time, it was met with enthusiasm and success.

At first, I didn't recognize that leadership is about playing the long game, seeing beyond the immediate, and working toward a sustainable impact. I, at times, was impatient and would feel as if my direct supervisor or peers did not want me to be successful. However, that is not always the case so as you lead there must be a level of maturity that develops. Everyone, regardless of how it may seem at times, is not out to stagnate your progress. It just might not be the right time. It could be the lack of financial resources or staff capacity as it is common that you must rely on others to bring your idea forward and be successful.

> Patience is not passive but it's an active exercise in perseverance and strategic thinking. It's understanding that sometimes you're planting seeds that won't bear fruit for years. And when those seeds finally sprout, the reward is far greater than if you had forced them to grow prematurely.

Humility in Leadership

There's also a lesson in humility. Ideas don't fail because they're inherently bad; sometimes, they fail because the environment isn't ready. Have you ever presented a proposal only to hear someone say, "We tried that three years ago, and it didn't work"? At first, it can feel like rejection or a dismissal of your creativity. More often than not, it's an indicator that the idea wasn't suited for the conditions at the time. Cultures evolve, and what once seemed impractical might become feasible as organizational dynamics shift.

One of my mentors shared a piece of wisdom that has stuck with me: "Not every 'no' is final. Sometimes, it's just a 'not now.'" This perspective has been invaluable. When faced with resistance, instead of giving up, I've learned to ask, "What conditions need to change for this idea to work?" By reframing the conversation, you move from frustration to curiosity and from defeat to determination. Leadership requires this kind of mental agility to transform setbacks into steppingstones and you'll quickly value this along the journey.

Collaboration: The Secret to Execution

Navigating the nuances of idea versus reality demands an acute understanding of your team's strengths and weaknesses. Leaders are not solitary visionaries; they're collaborators. It's essential to leverage the unique talents within your team to bring ideas to life. For instance, I once co-led a project aimed at streamlining processes across multiple departments. The task was daunting, and the initial plan was overly ambitious. By breaking the project into smaller, manageable components and aligning each with the expertise of specific team members, we were able to make steady progress. The result wasn't perfection – as it took 14 months to accomplish – but it was impactful and laid the groundwork for future improvements.

Industry research supports this collaborative approach. According to a Gallup study, teams that effectively utilize their members' strengths experience a 12.5% increase in productivity.[2] This underscores the importance of aligning ideas not just with organizational goals but also with the capabilities of the people executing them. As leaders, our role is to provide the vision while vision carriers (people who understand and are committed to the goal) bring it to life.

The Power of Humor in Leadership

Humor can be a powerful tool in bridging the gap between aspiration and reality. Leadership is serious work, yet it doesn't have to be absent of joy. I remember a particularly challenging budget meeting where tensions were high after discussing we had to cut funding. After a frustrating exchange, I said, "Well, at least we can't cut Starbucks. I'd be atrocious without my White Chocolate Mocha in the morning!" The room erupted in laughter, and the mood lightened just enough for us to tackle the tough decisions ahead. Humor humanizes leadership, reminding everyone—yourself included—that perfection isn't the goal. Progress is.

As you advance on your journey, embrace the duality of ideas and reality. Recognize that every challenge is an opportunity to learn, grow, and refine your approach. Be patient with the process and persistent in your pursuit of excellence. Understand that timing, collaboration, and resilience are just as critical as vision and ambition.

Leadership requires courage and resilience. It is deeply rewarding offering the chance to build meaningful relationships, create lasting change, and leave a legacy that outlives your tenure. Dream big, stay grounded, lead with conviction, and remain flexible. And most importantly, never stop learning. For it's in the interplay of ideas and reality that true leadership takes shape.

CHAPTER THREE
Building Confidence in Risks

"A risk not taken is a lesson not learned."

James stood at the open door of the plane, heart pounding, every instinct screaming at him to turn back. Below him, the earth stretched endlessly, a patchwork of greens and browns, so far away it felt almost unreal. The instructor's voice was steady behind him saying, "Trust your training. Trust yourself." But that was easier said than done. He had watched countless videos, practiced the form, and memorized every step of the jump, yet at this moment, none of that quieted the fear gripping his chest. The decision was his alone. No one could push him. No one could guarantee the perfect landing. The only way to move forward was to take the leap. With one deep breath, James closed his eyes, silenced the doubt, and stepped into the sky.

The freefall was chaos at first—wind roaring in his ears, gravity pulling him downward at an unrelenting speed. Then something changed. His training kicked in. He stabilized, spread his arms, and felt control settle in where panic once lived. The fear didn't disappear; it transformed into focus and exhilaration. As he pulled the parachute cord, the sudden jolt reminded him of something powerful: the risk had always been there, but so was the reward.

Reflecting on my journey as a leader, I've realized there were pivotal moments when I delayed taking action—moments that could have propelled my career and enriched my life. Like James in the story, leadership is no different than parachuting from a plane. The hardest part is stepping out, trusting yourself despite the fear, and embracing the unknown. When you do, you don't just fall—you fly. When you don't take risks, they became missed opportunities or delayed lessons.

Delaying Personal Aspirations

When I earned my doctorate, I envisioned a future immersed in teaching and research. I saw myself working closely with students, diving into their experiences, and contributing meaningfully to the academic discourse on student retention. Yet, despite my passion, I hesitated. I convinced myself there would be a better time, a perfect moment to act. And so, I waited.

> **As a leader, it's easy to lose sight of personal goals while chasing organizational ones. Don't.**

We often think our legacy hinges on the immediate impact we make in our roles. But what about the dreams that stir our hearts? What about the aspirations that once motivated us to embark on this journey? Neglecting these can lead to stagnation, not just for ourselves but for the people and organizations we aim to inspire.

After earning my doctorate, I was eager to continue the research I had started in the two-year college space, building on my work in four-year institutions. I wanted to uncover the nuances, identify the gaps, and contribute to meaningful solutions. Yet, year after year, I found reasons to postpone. Work consumed me, and excuses became my refuge. "Next year," I'd say, until years turned into nearly a decade. As

I write this now, that research remains dormant, a stark reminder of how easily we can sideline what truly matters.

This isn't just my story; it's a shared experience among leaders at every stage. Whether just starting or experienced in your career, there's a tendency to prioritize everything but ourselves. The consequences of delaying our aspirations are real. They haunt us, gnawing at the edges of our confidence, whispering "what if" during moments of quiet reflection. But here's the truth: the perfect moment doesn't exist. There's no ideal time to act, no guarantee of readiness. The only certainty is the present, and every day you wait is a day lost.

Learning from the Risk Takers

Take inspiration from Dorothy Steel, who found fame at 92 when she was cast in *Black Panther*. Her journey to becoming an actress wasn't without its setbacks or doubts, but she didn't let age or circumstance define her. She took the risk, embraced the opportunity, and delivered a performance that inspired millions. Dorothy's story is a powerful reminder that it's never too late to chase your dreams. What's stopping you from doing the same?

Looking back, I see how my hesitations stemmed from fear. Fear of failure, fear of judgment, and sometimes, fear of success. I doubted whether I was ready, whether I knew enough, or whether the timing was right. But let me tell you—those fears are thieves, robbing us of progress and potential. It's like the Nike slogan says: Just do it. Do it scared, do it unsure, do it imperfectly. What matters the most is that you start.

Every day is a new chance to step into the unknown. It's also a reminder of our finite time. Who decides when the right moment is? What if that moment is now? As leaders, we must resist the urge to wait for the stars to align. The world will move forward with or without us, so why not make today the day you begin?

Four Steps to Overcome Hesitation

You might be wondering, *"Okay, but how do I actually move forward?"* I'm glad you asked! Taking action—especially when uncertainty and fear creep in—can be daunting. But leadership requires movement. Stagnation will only keep you stuck where you are, while small, intentional steps will propel you toward your goals.

Here are four practical steps to break through hesitation and move forward with confidence:

1. **Start Small with Low-Risk Actions**
2. **Set Clear, Measurable Milestones**
3. **Create an Accountability System**
4. **Reframe Your View of Failure**

These steps will help you build momentum, strengthen your leadership, and ensure that hesitation does not keep you from stepping into your full potential.

Step 1: Start Small with Low-Risk Actions

The fear of failure can make any risk feel overwhelming, causing hesitation that paralyzes progress. The best way to counteract this fear is by starting small. Taking manageable steps minimizes pressure while still building momentum.

For example, if you're considering a career change, don't start by quitting your job—begin by researching industries, connecting with professionals in your desired field, or enrolling in a short online course to develop new skills. These low-risk actions reduce intimidation while positioning you for bigger moves down the line.

Small wins build confidence, and confidence fuels action. Every small step you take is an investment in a bigger outcome.

Step 2: Set Clear, Measurable Milestones

Without clear markers of progress, it's easy to feel like you're moving in circles. Setting **specific, measurable milestones** helps you track success, stay motivated, and make adjustments along the way. Research shows that writing down your goals significantly increases the likelihood of achieving them.

When writing this book, I didn't just sit down and start typing chapter after chapter. Instead, I spent months brainstorming, capturing ideas, and outlining key concepts—on paper, in my iPhone notes, and even on a dry-erase board. Slowly, the structure emerged, turning fragmented thoughts into a well-organized framework. While writing another book felt daunting at first, achieving small milestones—one chapter at a time—made the overall task feel manageable.

What milestones can you set to keep yourself on track? Write them down and celebrate the progress you make.

Step 3: Build an Accountability System

Taking risks can feel isolating, but having the right people in your corner can make all the difference. **Accountability turns dreams into action** by creating external motivation to keep moving forward. Surround yourself with individuals who challenge you, check in on your progress, and provide support when you need it most.

When writing this book, I consistently bounced ideas off my friends and colleagues to ensure clarity and impact. Their encouragement reinforced my commitment, and knowing that people were anticipating the final product kept me accountable. The more you engage others in your journey, the harder it becomes to abandon your progress.

Ask yourself: *Who in my life can hold me accountable?* It could be a mentor, a peer, or even a community of like-minded individuals striving toward similar goals.

Step 4: Reframe Your View of Failure

Many people remain stuck because they fear failure. They see it as a setback rather than what it truly is: a **learning opportunity**.

Every misstep, every detour, and every unexpected outcome carries a lesson that brings you closer to success. If you launch a new project and it doesn't go as planned, don't view it as a wasted effort. Instead, use the experience to **gather feedback, analyze what went wrong, and adjust your approach moving forward**. This shift in mindset allows you to take calculated risks without being paralyzed by the fear of "losing."

The most successful leaders are not those who have never failed but those who have **learned how to fail forward**. Every setback is an opportunity for refinement.

By applying these four steps—**starting small, setting measurable milestones, building accountability, and reframing failure**—you'll avoid stagnation and create a clear, actionable path toward personal and professional growth.

Let me share with you how I've applied these principles in my own life.

My Journey: From Hesitation to Action

I recall the long road to my doctorate. After earning my master's, I knew I wanted more—not just for the credentials but for the knowledge and doors it would open. I envisioned myself as a university president or CEO, equipped to lead with both expertise and vision. It took me eight years to finally take that next step. During that time, I watched others embrace opportunities I let slip by—not due to a lack of qualifications, rather my own hesitation.

Even after earning my doctorate, I hesitated to pursue programs that would prepare me for executive leadership. I would research fellowships, gather information, and then let deadlines pass. Doubt crept in, convincing me there was always next year.

Finally, I decided enough was enough and restarted the process of exploring programs—**starting small**. I gathered information on 6–8 programs and discussed experiences with colleagues and mentors. **Setting measurable milestones**, I gradually narrowed down my options based on application timelines. This process took a few months.

During that time, I had conversations with close friends and colleagues about my goals and options. Through these discussions, a sense of interest and accountability developed. As they understood my direction and reasons for pursuing it, their support helped keep me on track, ultimately **forming an accountability system**.

After narrowing down the program, I applied and anxiously waited to see the outcome. When I shared my plan with a mentor, they expressed skepticism: "I don't think they'll accept you. They only seem to accept executive-level leaders." Their words were humbling and at the same time ignited a fire within me. It reminded me of a moment in college when the Dean of the School of Business told me I couldn't secure an internship in my program.

At the time, I felt defeated and nearly accepted his words as my reality. But instead of walking through the doors already created—established internships—I built my own opportunity. Partnering with an agency that had no prior connection to the program, I carved my own path. That semester, I completed a rewarding internship, received glowing reviews, and proved to the Dean that I had what it took to succeed.

While the leadership program felt like a different challenge, it carried the same lesson: I had to try and refuse to let someone else's opinion define my reality. This mindset helped me **reframe the idea of failure**. I'm proud to say I submitted my application—and to my surprise, I was accepted.

That experience taught me two key lessons:

1. You miss 100% of the shots you don't take.
2. Opposition isn't always a barrier; sometimes, it's a test of your resolve.

As leaders, we must embrace the risks and uncertainties that come with pursuing our dreams. Every setback is an opportunity to refine our strategy and grow stronger.

The Power of Purpose

> Remember, leadership is as much about self-investment as it is about serving others. We should consider our divine purpose and take intentional steps to fulfill it.

Over the years, I've often shared an analogy about conception—that our journey begins long before we take our first breath. During conception, a series of intricate, almost miraculous events unfold. Paths cross, choices are made, and within our mother's womb, a single egg is fertilized, becoming us. In that moment, the question *"Why do we exist?"* lies dormant, waiting for its time to surface.

We are not accidents. From the very start, our existence has been purposeful, woven into a grander design. At some point in our lives, we come to understand this truth: we were not created by chance; we were designed with intention and born with the potential to shape the world around us.

Our lives are not mere coincidences—they are profound opportunities to make a difference. Whether through innovation, mentorship, or advocacy, our impact matters. But we cannot create that impact if we are paralyzed by fear or distracted by excuses.

So, I ask you: *What are you waiting for?* What's holding you back from writing that book, launching that project, or applying for that dream role? Don't let the years slip by. Take the first step and make up your mind to just do it. It doesn't have to be perfect—it just has to be sincere.

As you navigate your leadership journey, keep this in mind: *Your time is now.* Embrace the challenges, learn from the setbacks, and celebrate the wins. Above all, trust yourself. You have everything you need to succeed—all that's left is to take the leap.

I'm cheering for you.

CHAPTER FOUR
The Watchful Eyes

> "Be careful not to give someone the ammunition they could use against you—protect your words, actions, and decisions."

One of my favorite songs from the 1980s is Rockwell's *"Somebody's Watching Me."* The hook, made unforgettable by Michael Jackson's haunting refrain, has stuck with me over the years: *"I always feel like somebody's watching me."* At the time, it was a clever ode to paranoia wrapped in a catchy melody. Today, it feels less like paranoia and more like prophecy. In an age of pervasive social media, where every post, like, and comment can be dissected by anyone with an internet connection, we live in a world where someone is *always* watching – and willing to provide their opinion.

Balancing Transparency and Discretion

I've always valued discretion. It's been a cornerstone of how I carry myself, both personally and professionally. At work, I made a conscious effort to share only what I felt was relevant, leaving other parts of my life intentionally private. It wasn't secrecy; it was balance—a deliberate boundary that kept me centered. But social media operates in a realm where such boundaries are easily blurred. Platforms like Facebook, Instagram, LinkedIn, and Twitter (now X) thrive on connection, inviting us to share, react, and engage with a vast network of people. While these spaces can foster incredible opportunities for leaders to connect with their communities, they also demand a level of vigilance many of us underestimate.

Initially, my online presence mirrored my professional life—measured and purposeful. I posted about my travels, shared thoughtful reflections, and highlighted the work I was passionate about. It felt authentic and aligned with my values. Yet, as I scrolled and clicked, I began to realize how effortlessly social media could draw you into its endless web. At times friends would send me funny clips or things for me to look at that they felt would be appealing to me. At times, it was, and other times it wasn't. Yet, it still allowed me to "click" and that is often how it starts. Algorithms serve you content tailored to your interests, luring you into interactions that, while seemingly harmless, leave a trail. A trail that others, particularly employers, might follow.

A Hard Lesson in Digital Awareness

The stakes became painfully clear during one of the most pivotal moments and lessons of my career. I was pursuing a leadership role that promised to be both challenging and rewarding. The process was rigorous—interviews, presentations, and candid conversations about what I could bring to the organization. Everything felt aligned until I received an unexpected email. They wanted to discuss something they had noticed on my social media.

The request caught me off guard. I had always been careful about my online behavior. I avoided controversial posts, refrained from engaging in heated debates, and steered clear of anything that could cast a shadow over my character. Still, I agreed to the call, eager to address whatever concerns they had.

When the call came, their concern wasn't about what I had posted or written. It was about the people I followed. "We noticed that some of the accounts you follow post seminude content," they said. Their tone was polite but firm, leaving no room for misinterpretation: this was a problem.

I was stunned. My mind raced to understand how something so peripheral could overshadow my qualifications. These weren't personal connections. Many were artists, entertainers, or public figures whose content had shifted over time. For instance, one was a musician I had followed for his work, only to see his account evolve into something more provocative. These days they call them "thirst traps" – posts that are sexually appealing to draw people into watching your material and get more likes and follows. They weren't mine, yet, here I was, defending myself against a perception I hadn't even considered.

A Lesson in Digital Breadcrumbs

This was a moment of reckoning. What I had dismissed as a minor oversight had become a glaring red flag in their eyes. It was sobering to realize that, to them, my digital footprint spoke louder than my words. And they weren't alone in this scrutiny.

I later discovered that 70% of employers now use social media to screen candidates,[3] with 54% admitting they've found content that led them to reject a candidate entirely.[4] Whoa, right? For younger generations who grew up documenting their lives online, this level of scrutiny might seem second nature. But for those of us who came of age before the digital era, it can feel invasive—even unfair.

I know firsthand that generational differences often shape how we view social media. I see it every time I try to chat with my mother on Facebook—she likes every post, comments on other people's comments, and has no idea what "Facebook Live" is. There's a clear distinction in how different generations use these platforms.

Millennials and Gen Z, for example, tend to see their online presence as an extension of themselves[5]—a space to express, connect, and advocate. In contrast, Baby Boomers and Gen X, who joined these platforms later in life, often view social media more as a tool than a personal stage.[6]

Yet, regardless of generational perspectives, one truth remains: leaders are judged not only by what they say and do in person but also by what they post and endorse online.

Lessons in Leadership and Social Media

This experience taught me an important lesson: *perception outweighs intent*. It didn't matter whether my actions were innocent or my associations incidental—in the eyes of others, especially those evaluating me for a leadership role, these details mattered.

> As leaders, we must recognize that our digital presence extends beyond us. It reflects on our organizations, our teams, and our values.

At a conference one year, I sat in the audience as a higher education executive shared a striking story. Her child's college had contacted her—not because of her child's social media activity, but because of her own. The institution was concerned that her online stance on certain issues could potentially impact its reputation. Naturally, this didn't sit well with her, nor should it have—her personal online presence had nothing to do with the institution. But after sharing her perspective and confronting their audacity, the conversation never resurfaced.

When I received **that** call, I made a decision. I took ownership of my actions and their consequences, even if they were unintended. I combed through my social media, unfollowed accounts that could be misconstrued, and adjusted my privacy settings. It wasn't about erasing my digital past; it was about ensuring my online presence aligned with the leader I strive to be.

Moving Forward with Intentionality

Leaders across industries have learned, sometimes the hard way like I did, that online presence can shape their careers just as much as their real-world actions. Elon Musk, for example, has repeatedly made headlines due to his tweets, influencing Tesla's stock price and public perception in both positive and negative ways. Likewise, former executives like John Schnatter of Papa John's found their reputations irreparably damaged due to controversial remarks – proving that words, even in fleeting moments, can have lasting consequences.

In my social media lesson, I learned that what you might click on – whether in the past, currently, or in the future could be looked at when considering professional opportunities. So, what does this mean for you as a leader? It's simple: proactive reputation management is non-negotiable.

> "Be careful not to give someone the ammunition they could use against you—protect your words, actions, and decisions."

As a leader, you have a responsibility to curate both your professional and personal images. In a world where the line between the two is increasingly blurred, intentionality is no longer optional—it's essential.

And while we each have our own digital footprint, working for a company often forces us to navigate the tension between personal authenticity and professional representation. It's a hard pill to swallow at times, yet a reality leaders must recognize.

As you reflect on what I just shared, consider these lessons:

1. Understand that your reputation is one of your greatest assets—protect it fiercely.

What you post, like, or follow on social media can be **amplified, scrutinized, and, at times, weaponized.** Before posting, commenting, or engaging with content, ask yourself: *Would I be comfortable seeing this on a billboard next to my name?* If the answer is no, reconsider your action. A moment of impulse can have lasting consequences.

2. Take ownership of your digital footprint.

Regularly audit your online presence—not out of fear, but out of respect for the roles you occupy and the people who look up to you. Early in my career, I made a personal rule not to connect with colleagues on Facebook. It was a boundary I set, though it sometimes became difficult to maintain.

After my own experience, I began **Googling myself regularly** and found old content from my college days. Nothing extreme, but things that could easily be cleaned up and deleted. I recommend you do the same. Seeing your digital presence through the lens of a future employer or client gives you the opportunity to **shape your narrative before someone else does.**

3. Embrace and set boundaries.

Oversharing might feel authentic in the moment, but it can invite **unnecessary scrutiny.** As leaders, we naturally form opinions on situations, events, and people—but publicly sharing them isn't always wise. Online words, even those spoken with good intentions, can be misinterpreted or used against us in the future.

Setting boundaries could mean having **separate accounts, private settings, or exercising thoughtful discretion.** Some people I know maintain private accounts under pseudonyms, allowing them the freedom to express themselves. However, **leaders often need to take a neutral stance** on certain issues—especially those that might provoke controversy or create long-term repercussions.

4. Remember that leadership is about growth, not perfection.

We all make mistakes—I certainly have. What defines us isn't the mistake itself, **but how we respond to it.** Don't wait for someone else to tell your story. Instead, proactively shape your personal brand. **Share valuable insights, thought leadership, and reflections that reinforce your credibility while amplifying your humanity.**

This journey has taught me **humility, resilience, and the importance of staying true to my values—even when the world is watching.** But staying true to my values doesn't mean broadcasting them every time someone asks, *"What do you think?"* on social media. Some conversations are best left unsaid.

There must always be a level of **poise and discretion in leadership.** In today's world, where perception shapes reality, protecting your digital reputation isn't just about avoiding mistakes—it's about **leading with intention, wisdom, and foresight.**

Protecting What You've Built

Think about the last time someone misjudged you based on limited information. How did it feel? Frustrating? Unfair? Now, imagine if that misjudgment wasn't just a one-time experience but a permanent label—etched into your reputation because of a single misstep.

Leadership means living under the opinions of others. Every action, every word, every decision—whether online or in person—has the potential to shape how others perceive you. The truth is **no one sets out to sabotage their own reputation.** Yet, carelessness, lack of foresight, or a single lapse in judgment can have lasting consequences.

Ask yourself:

- Are you intentional in how you present yourself, both online and offline?
- Do your values align with the way you show up in the world?
- If someone who had never met you formed an opinion based on your social media alone, would they see a leader worth following?

A strong reputation isn't built overnight—but it can be shattered in an instant. Moving forward, consider your reputation not just as something to manage, but as an asset to invest in. Every interaction, every choice, and every shared moment is an opportunity to reinforce who you are and what you stand for.

Whether you're a new or experienced leader, our lives are often under a magnifying glass. That scrutiny can feel daunting, yet it also presents an opportunity. By owning our narratives, embracing transparency, and learning from our missteps, we become not only better leaders but also better human beings. After all, leadership isn't just about guiding others; it's about continually growing ourselves.

In a world that is always watching—but more importantly, always remembering—what do you want it to remember about you? Let your actions, regardless of the platform or stage, reflect the leader you aspire to be.

PART TWO: PURPOSEFUL LEADERSHIP ADVICE

The strength
of a bridge
is found
in the materials
used to make it.

CHAPTER FIVE
Navigating the Critics

> "As you climb, realize that everyone won't support your rope."

Growing up, my mother often reminded me, *"Everyone isn't your friend."* It was one of those lessons that stuck with me, though it took several painful experiences for it to truly sink in. As a child, I believed that anyone who was nice to me had good intentions and genuinely wanted to know me. In my mind, they could be my buddy, my confidant, or even my cheerleader. Although, life has a way of teaching us the lessons we stubbornly resist. Sure, some people will be in your corner, rooting for your success, but others will stand across the street, watching and waiting for you to fail.

This lesson, while valuable in childhood, became indispensable in my journey as a leader. Leadership, I've discovered, is a paradox. On one hand, it's about building relationships, fostering trust, and inspiring others. On the other, it's about navigating a landscape where not everyone shares your vision or intentions. During my time leading a social organization, this paradox was laid bare. It was a role I embraced with pride and dedication, pouring countless hours into creating a strategic vision, fostering engagement, and aligning our organization for the future. Yet, it was also one of the most challenging periods of my life.

The Illusion of Unlimited Trust

Leadership often comes with its share of status and respect. At the time, I was perceived as someone stable—professionally, financially, and mentally. While these perceptions weren't entirely wrong, they also painted a target on my back. People assumed I could help everyone, that I had the answers, and that my support came without limits. Naively, I believed the same. I trusted that those I supported would have my best interests at heart, that they'd value my intentions and reciprocate my trust. That belief, I've learned, can be a dangerous one.

One incident stands out as a defining moment in my leadership journey. A member faced a significant crisis. He needed $1,000 to address an issue that, without intervention, could have had dire consequences. At the time, I was financially stable enough to help, and I wanted to make a difference. He assured me of his credibility, and I, wanting to believe the best in people, extended the loan. *"If you can't afford to lose it, you can't afford to loan it."* That's the wisdom I ignored. Predictably, I never saw that money again. The sting of the financial loss was sharp. It paled in comparison to the deeper hurt of misplaced trust. His character, which had been vouched for, didn't align with his actions. While the loss was frustrating, it taught me an invaluable lesson about boundaries and discernment.

The Importance of Boundaries

As a leader, you quickly learn that not everyone you engage with is meant to be close to you. Boundaries are essential for maintaining your own sanity while also preserving the trust and productivity of those you lead. If trust is breached it can ripple outward affecting your relationships and the culture of your team or organization. In this instance, people were watching to see how I'd respond. And let me tell you, it wasn't easy. There were moments when I felt frustrated, moments when I thought, *"This isn't fair."* But fairness, as I've come to understand, is a luxury in leadership. It's not always about what's fair; it's about what's right. As Michelle Obama wisely said, *"When they go low, you go high."*

The lesson I took away was this: establish boundaries, be discerning about trust, and recognize that every challenge carries a lesson. A stark reality is that growth comes from the experiences you encounter along the way, and while guiding others is an essential part of leadership, equally important is the ability to guide yourself. Sometimes, the moments that sting the most are the ones that lead to the greatest growth.

The Rope of Leadership

Another important realization is captured perfectly in the saying, *"As you climb, realize everyone won't support your rope."* The climb is rewarding and isolating. Not everyone will cheer for you, and some might even loosen the knots in your rope when you're not looking. As a leader, I experienced this firsthand. From social media scrutiny to behind-the-scenes politics, the challenges were unrelenting.

Reflecting on these moments, I've come to appreciate the value of discernment in leadership. Discernment in whom you trust, what you share, and how you navigate relationships. Leadership, I've learned, is as much about the company you keep as it is about the goals you pursue. Gossip, for example, is a subtle yet powerful force in any organization. I've always been amazed at how quickly information travels, often distorting along the way. Avoiding entanglement in the rumor mill isn't just about safeguarding your reputation; it's about fostering a culture of respect and trust. Being selective about whom you confide in and exercising tact in conversations are practices that safeguard your reputation and career stability.

Equally important is recognizing the agendas of others. Leadership often involves aligning people toward a shared vision; except, everyone's priorities will not align with yours. Some individuals may prioritize personal gain over collective progress. I've witnessed this more times than I'd like to admit. The key is to stay grounded in the needs of the people you lead. By keeping their well-being and goals at the forefront, you're better equipped to navigate competing agendas and stay true to your purpose.

Navigating Politics with Integrity

Lastly, politics – a topic that I must take some time to discuss because of its impact. Leadership often brings an uncomfortable realization: **politics are inescapable.** They're woven into the fabric of organizations, influencing decisions and dynamics in ways that aren't always visible. Early in my journey, I resisted this idea, believing I could rise above the chaos. Yet leadership has a way of forcing you to confront things you'd rather avoid. At some point, you must face the politics head-on, and when you do, **navigate them with integrity.**

Understanding power structures, observing dynamics, and managing relationships strategically have all been invaluable tools in my growth as a leader. But I can't lie to you—navigating workplace politics is one of the most challenging, yet necessary, aspects of leadership.

What Are Workplace Politics?

Workplace politics refers to the power dynamics, informal networks, and unspoken rules that influence decision-making within an organization. They exist in **every** workplace—whether acknowledged or not. Politics shape **who gets promoted, which initiatives receive funding, and how conflicts are resolved.** Sometimes, these dynamics operate in the open, but more often, they exist beneath the surface.

If you've ever witnessed a good idea get dismissed, not because it lacked merit, but because the "wrong person" presented it, you've witnessed office politics at play. If you've seen someone rise through the ranks due to strategic alliances rather than skill, that's politics too. **It's not always fair, but it is always present.**

Why Leaders Can't Ignore Politics

Many new leaders make the mistake of thinking they can **avoid** workplace politics altogether. I was one of them. I assumed that as long as I worked hard, focused on results and treated people well, I wouldn't have to engage in the political landscape. Unfortunately **ignoring politics doesn't make them disappear—it just puts you at a disadvantage.**

I learned this lesson the hard way. Years ago, I attended the graduation ceremony of a program I had worked tirelessly to help launch. This program wasn't just an idea I had supported—it was something I had poured countless hours into. I collaborated with partners across the country, navigated complex approval processes, compiled applications, gathered data, and aligned everything necessary for official approval. The program had taken off successfully, and that day, we were gathered to celebrate its first graduating class—the tangible proof of our efforts.

As I sat in the audience, I watched as various people were acknowledged for their contributions. Leaders, staff members, and frontline workers all received their well-earned recognition. But something became painfully clear: **my name wasn't among them.**

Because I wasn't on the frontline working directly with participants, the behind-the-scenes efforts that brought the program to life were overlooked. It wasn't that I expected a standing ovation, but as I listened to the long list of thank-yous, my name—and my contributions—were never mentioned. The absence of recognition wasn't just an oversight; it was a political moment, an unspoken statement about visibility, influence, and how credit is distributed within an organization.

At first, I felt frustrated. But as I sat there, I realized this was bigger than me—it was a lesson in institutional politics. **I hadn't positioned myself in a way that made my contributions undeniable.** I had done the work, but I had failed to ensure that my role in the program's success was recognized.

After the ceremony, an executive leader walked over to me. They looked around and then asked, *"Why were you sitting over here and not with the rest of the staff?"*

I responded honestly: *"I wasn't invited to sit with everyone."*

They shook their head and said something that stuck with me: *"Weren't you the one who got this program approved?"*

That single moment of recognition was validating, but it also exposed a deeper truth—**I had failed to navigate the politics of visibility.** By not advocating for my role, I had unintentionally created a culture where people assumed I could be overlooked.

From that point forward, I made a conscious decision: **I wouldn't let my work speak for itself—I would speak for my work.**

I began proactively ensuring that key stakeholders knew my contributions to initiatives and strategies. I didn't boast or demand credit, but I did become more strategic in making my presence known—whether through regular updates to leadership, ensuring my name was attached to critical documentation, or simply being more vocal about my involvement in projects.

That experience taught me something invaluable: **You don't have to play dirty, but you do have to play smart.** Leadership isn't just about doing the work—it's about ensuring that work is seen and valued by the right people. Because in organizations, credit doesn't always go to those who deserve it; it often goes to those who understand the politics of recognition.

How Politics Influence Decision-Making

Every decision in an organization—whether hiring a new leader, launching a project, or allocating resources—is influenced by **power dynamics, relationships, and competing interests.** Leaders who understand these forces make **informed** decisions, while those who ignore them find themselves constantly blindsided.

I want you to think about it like this: Imagine you're playing chess but refuse to acknowledge your opponent's strategy. No matter how well you move your pieces, you'll still lose. Your goal isn't just to look at the corner in front of you, but to anticipate what lies beyond it. The same applies to leadership—if you're unaware of the political landscape, you'll find yourself outmaneuvered, frustrated, and ineffective.

But politics aren't inherently bad. When approached with **integrity and awareness,** they can be navigated in ways that build trust, create alignment, and advance meaningful work. The key is **knowing how to engage without compromising your values.**

How to Navigate Workplace Politics with Integrity

1. Develop Political Awareness Without Becoming Political

There's a difference between **understanding** politics and **being consumed** by them. Strong leaders develop **political intelligence**—the ability to recognize power structures, alliances, and unspoken rules—without compromising their character.

Ask yourself:

- Who are the real decision-makers in my organization?
- What are their priorities, and how do they align with mine?
- Where do informal power structures exist, and how do they shape outcomes?

Being politically aware allows you to navigate conversations, gain buy-in, and **position yourself strategically without manipulation.**

2. Build Relationships Before You Need Them

Some leaders only engage with key players when they need a favor. That's a mistake. Strong leaders build **genuine** relationships **before** they need anything. One thing I've attempted to do when entering into a new role or having a new leader come into a new role is connect them with people within the organization for relationship building. The worst position to be in is to need something and not know who you should talk to.

Make it a habit to cultivate relationships across all levels of your organization—not just for political advantage, but because **strong networks create stronger leaders.**

3. Observe Before You Engage

Not every battle is worth fighting. **Before inserting yourself into workplace politics, take time to observe.** Who holds influence? What unspoken rules govern interactions? Who are the gatekeepers?

Imagine stepping into a new organization and immediately taking sides in a long-standing debate without fully understanding the history. Don't do that, **that's a recipe for disaster.** Strong leaders don't rush to align themselves with factions—they **listen, learn, and assess before acting.**

4. Speak with Precision, Not Emotion

Politics often thrive on **emotionally charged reactions.** When faced with conflict, resist the urge to **react** impulsively. Instead, **respond** strategically.

I once witnessed a leader lose credibility in a single meeting. He had been overlooked for a promotion and, instead of addressing it professionally, he let his emotions take over—venting frustrations publicly. The moment he lost control, he lost influence – quickly.

The best leaders **stay composed, choose their words carefully, and engage strategically.** If you feel emotional, step back, take a breath, and approach the conversation when you can **control the narrative.**

5. Stay True to Your Values

Perhaps the most important lesson: **Politics will test your integrity.** You will see people cut corners, make unethical decisions, and leverage relationships for self-serving gain. You may even feel pressured to do the same.

Don't.

There is a way to **navigate politics without losing yourself.** Align your decisions with your values. Advocate for fairness. Be transparent when possible, and always act in a way that allows you to sleep at night. Integrity doesn't mean avoiding politics—it means **engaging with wisdom and ethics.**

Hold Yourself Accountable

Accountability and leadership always go hand in hand. When you're in a position of authority, people naturally take an interest in who you are and what you stand for. This "law of attraction," if you're not careful, can lead to an environment filled with imposters. As an adult, who you let into your circle is ultimately your decision. And no matter how cautious you are, there will inevitably be times when you get it wrong. Honestly, it's unavoidable. So, when that happens, own your narrative—even when it's uncomfortable—and make the necessary adjustments with tact.

A Lesson from My Mom

Let me share a story with you. When I was younger, I used to raise an eyebrow every time my mom realized she had made the wrong decision. She'd mutter, "I am so stupid. I should've known better!" And then, with her usual resilience, she'd follow it up with a sigh and say, *"Oh, well. I know better for next time."* It used to confuse me, but over time, I understood something important. My mom wasn't being harsh on herself—she was holding herself accountable. She recognized the mistake, owned it, and instead of dwelling on regret, she was learning and moving forward.

One year, I saw this accountability in action when she called me, frantic and flustered. A man from a sweepstakes had contacted her, insisting she needed to pay $300. He created a sense of urgency, making her feel like she had no other option. One thing he told her was that she couldn't tell anyone. Despite this, she still wanted me to talk to him and make sense of the situation.

I wasn't able to pick up the phone right away, but when I called her back, she was still excited about what was happening. As she shared the details, I quickly realized she'd fallen for a scam. I asked a few questions, and it became clear. The man had tricked her into giving him $300 in hopes of winning $1,000,000. By the time we figured it out, the money was already gone, and there was nothing we could do to get it back.

In that moment, I heard the familiar words: *"I am so stupid. I should've known better."* But instead of letting her stay in self-blame, I gently reminded her that it was okay. Yes, it was a mistake, but it was one she could learn from. *"We know better now,"* I told her. *"We won't let it happen again."*

I share this with you because, just like my mom, you might find yourself in situations where you're your biggest critic. And that's okay—what's important is that you focus on the things that protect your integrity and your leadership.

Not everyone deserves a place in your circle.

The people around you, your support system, should guide and uplift you. They should help you grow and keep you grounded. But remember, in leadership, everyone won't always be there to hold your ladder or support your rope. That's a tough truth, yet one that's essential to understand. Not everyone will have your back, and that's part of the journey.

As you climb, you'll face moments where the rope may fray, or the knots might loosen. You'll encounter obstacles that challenge your path and force you to reevaluate your decisions. With each pull, each step forward, you're becoming stronger. You're becoming more resilient. And, just like my mom learned, you'll grow more compassionate with every lesson. Mistakes may be made, but they will shape you into the leader you're meant to be. And that, my friend, is a victory in itself.

CHAPTER SIX
The Collaborative North Star

> "When we dream, we unlock the key to our innermost potential. When we share, we expose others to what could be. But when we act, we unleash the power to accomplish what once seemed impossible."

Want to hear something funny? I wrote this chapter, then scrapped it and started over. Why? Because you deserved more. More insight into the power of dreaming. More understanding of how vision shapes the workplace and personal growth. More clarity on how it fuels us as human beings. A leadership book without a dedicated focus on vision would feel incomplete. And let's face it, no one wants to settle for something that feels unfinished.

I began this chapter with a simple but powerful reflection:

"When we dream, we unlock the key to our innermost potential. When we share, we expose others to what could be. But when we act, we unleash the power to accomplish what once seemed impossible."

I wrote these words while reflecting on the role vision plays in motivation and inspiration. Think about the moments when you felt a deep connection to a cause. The excitement, the energy, the willingness to go the extra mile. The way you rallied others to join you on the journey. Dreams—closely tied to vision—create that momentum. They fuel the leader who dares to share their purpose and inspire others to believe in something bigger than themselves.

Direction, Focus, and the Power of a Clear Vision

Leading people without a clear direction is like running a race with no finish line. What good is the work if you don't know where you're heading? A mentor of mine, who is also my pastor, often says, *"If you don't know where you're going, you'll probably end up somewhere else."* For me, nothing irritates me more than to be on a trip, lost, and won't ask anyone for directions. These are your directions.

When we have a vision—especially a clear one—it is powerful. The ability to envision what could be shapes us and provides the foundation for impactful leadership. I believe dreams ignite passion. Passion evolves into vision. Vision provides direction. Direction leads to action. Action produces results. In this chapter, I'll show you why that matters and how to bring it to life.

The Emotional Investment in Vision

There is something deeply personal about dreaming. Have you ever had a dream so vivid, so exhilarating, that you woke up feeling like you could conquer the world? I have. And that feeling of surge and belief, carries over into leadership.

A leader who is deeply connected to their vision tackles challenges with energy and enthusiasm. They don't just see obstacles; they see opportunities to rise above them. That passion fuels persistence, turning exhaustion into motivation and setbacks into lessons. The work no longer feels like a duty—it becomes a calling.

I once knew a woman who woke up before sunrise every morning, not because she had to, but because she couldn't wait to get started on a project she believed would change lives. She worked in education, and after years of watching students struggle with financial barriers, she developed a program to help underprivileged students gain access to scholarships, career mentorship, and real-world internships. She wasn't just doing a job—she was building a bridge for students who might have otherwise been overlooked.

She spent late nights researching funding opportunities, sending emails, and making phone calls, often sacrificing sleep just to push the initiative forward. When setbacks came, she adjusted. When roadblocks appeared, she found another way through. What drove her? The vision of a student, one who might have given up, instead walking across a stage with a diploma in hand, ready to take on the world.

That's what vision does. It wakes you up early and keeps you up late, not out of obligation, but because you can't imagine giving up on something so meaningful. It fuels action and transforms ideas into realities that impact lives.

But, what happens when a personal vision doesn't align with a collaborative one?

A Personal Lesson in Leadership and Vision

When I stepped into my role as a department head, I had already earned my degree in business management and understood the importance of organizational vision. I had studied mission statements, strategic goals, and leadership principles, and I carried that foundation into my work. I leaned on my institution's mission to guide our department, focusing our efforts on key initiatives that aligned with our broader goals.

Everything seemed to be falling into place. I introduced a concept called *Raising the B.A.R.*—reducing Barriers, increasing Access to resources, and Refining processes to make them more equitable for students. The idea caught on, and our team made remarkable progress. We created specialized teams, tracked our outcomes, and built momentum that made us feel unstoppable.

Then everything shifted. Organizational priorities changed, and my role expanded. Suddenly, I was no longer responsible for just one department but multiple areas, each with its own unique challenges. What once felt like a well-oiled machine now seemed like a scattered puzzle. I found myself at a crossroads, struggling to merge different teams and functions into a unified vision.

It wasn't easy. But challenges are often opportunities in disguise. And as I would come to learn, vision isn't just about setting a course—it's about adapting, refining, and ensuring that no matter the obstacles, you continue moving forward.

But what exactly is vision? It is not just about throwing ideas at the wall and hoping something sticks. Real vision requires strategy, intention, and a commitment to meaningful impact.

The Anatomy of Vision: What It Is and What It Isn't

Growing up in the church, I would hear many profound messages, but one came from the bible in Proverbs 29:18, *"Where there is no vision, the people perish."* As simple as that is, the weight of it means so much.

We probably can agree that having a vision is essential. But, what are characteristics you can look for in one? An impactful vision brings clarity of purpose. It ensures that everyone on the team understands their role and how their contributions fit into the larger picture. Without this clarity, team members can feel lost or unmotivated, leading to inefficiencies and wasted resources. Conversely, a shared vision aligns the team, fostering collaboration and driving productivity. Studies show that only 36% of U.S. employees are engaged in their work.[7] However, engagement is closely tied to organizational success—and a clear vision plays a crucial role. When employees understand how their roles contribute to the organization's vision, they are more likely to be engaged and committed.[8]

Before we move on, let's address the elephant in the room. Leadership, like everything else, has two sides. We often believe we know exactly what a strong vision looks like—until we realize we don't. It's like assembling furniture without the instructions. It seems simple at first, but suddenly, you're left with extra screws and no idea where they belong.

Let's clear things up by breaking down what makes a vision truly effective—and just as importantly, what and when it is not.

What a Good Vision Is

A compelling vision inspires and engages. When people believe in a shared goal, they feel a sense of belonging and purpose that energizes their work. A strong vision acts as a rallying cry, motivating individuals to innovate, collaborate, and commit to the team's success. It aligns efforts, providing clarity on the "why" behind the work, which fosters deeper investment from team members.

A well-defined vision also serves as a strategic framework for decision-making. It helps leaders stay proactive rather than reactive, ensuring that choices align with long-term goals rather than short-term fixes. Organizations with clearly articulated visions are better equipped to adapt to market shifts and seize new opportunities—an essential advantage in today's fast-changing world.

Additionally, a good vision fosters adaptability and resilience. Change is inevitable, and teams without a clear direction can become stagnant or resistant to it. But, when a vision is strong, it provides a sense of stability even amid uncertainty. It empowers teams to embrace challenges as opportunities for growth, rather than obstacles that derail progress.

Here are five key attributes of an effective strategic vision statement:[9]

1. **Future-Oriented** – Envisioning long-term success and impact.
2. **Inspiring & Challenging** – Encouraging growth beyond comfort zones.
3. **Motivating & Memorable** – Resonating emotionally and intellectually.
4. **Purpose-driven** – Rooted in core values and organizational identity.
5. **Unique** – Distinctly tailored to the team and its mission.

What a Good Vision is Not

A vision is not just a vague statement or a set of empty words on a company website. It must be actionable, guiding both leadership and frontline teams in their daily decisions. A vision without alignment to real work becomes meaningless, leaving employees disengaged and uninspired.

A vision is also not a rigid blueprint that resists change. While it should provide direction, it must allow for adaptability. Leaders who hold onto an outdated vision without considering evolving needs risk stifling innovation and limiting their team's potential.

Lastly, a vision is not a solo endeavor. It cannot be dictated from the top without input or buy-in from those responsible for bringing it to life. A vision that lacks inclusivity often fails to resonate, leading to misalignment, low morale, and resistance to change. Instead, a strong vision is shared, understood, and embraced at every level, creating a culture of unity and purpose.

Why is this important? Well, I experienced a similar situation where a unit lacked a clear vision, and the mistake forced me to look inwardly to develop a solution.

Navigating Change and Defining Vision

One thing I have learned in management is that change never stops. No matter how well-structured a plan may seem, agility remains essential. As I advanced in my career, I found myself in a unique position—leading a team that excelled operationally but lacked a clear, collaborative vision. The absence of direction gnawed at me. While the institution and division had overarching visions, my department struggled to establish its own identity.

It was a challenging place to be, caught between the expectations of my direct supervisor and the needs of my team. Looking back, I realized that in my effort to align with my supervisor's vision, I had overlooked something just as important—creating a vision that gave my team a sense of purpose and direction.

This experience reinforced a valuable lesson: clarity is everything. Without a clear vision, our goals felt scattered, and our efforts lacked cohesion. Recognizing the problem, I committed to addressing it head-on. Over time, as I navigated changes across different units, I learned how to work within the "grey areas" to unify our efforts. And it all started with a proper assessment—identifying areas for improvement and finding ways to amplify impact.

Through multiple iterations of this process, I developed the *Collaborative North Star Framework*—a guiding principle centered on teamwork and partnership. I want to introduce this framework to you at a very high level, but at its core, it helps leaders identify the common threads that connect both similar and diverse units to foster a shared vision.

The Collaborative North Star: A Framework for Transformational Leadership

The Leadership Gap: Why Teams Struggle

Leadership goes beyond setting goals and making decisions. It requires bringing people together in a way that creates lasting collaboration, trust, and impact. Many teams struggle not because they lack talent or resources but because they lack alignment. People work hard but often in disconnected ways, pulling in different directions instead of moving forward together.

This lack of cohesion leads to frustration, inefficiency, and a culture where individual efforts outweigh collective success. Leaders see the signs—miscommunication, low engagement, competing priorities—but without a structured approach, the problem persists.

The **Collaborative North Star Framework** provides a roadmap for leaders who want to transform their teams from loosely connected individuals into a unified force. It moves organizations from fragmented teamwork to a **shared vision, strong relationships, and seamless collaboration.**

What is the Collaborative North Star Framework?

The Collaborative North Star Framework is a structured approach to leadership that focuses on these core outcomes:

1. **Establishing a Shared Vision** – A clear and compelling direction that unites the team.
2. **Amplifying Trust** – A culture where transparency and accountability strengthen relationships.
3. **Enhancing Teamwork** – Seamless handoffs between roles, responsibilities, and leadership changes.

When these elements work together, teams develop clarity, connection, and confidence. The framework ensures that every member understands their role, trusts their colleagues, and moves forward with a sense of purpose rather than reacting to obstacles as they arise.

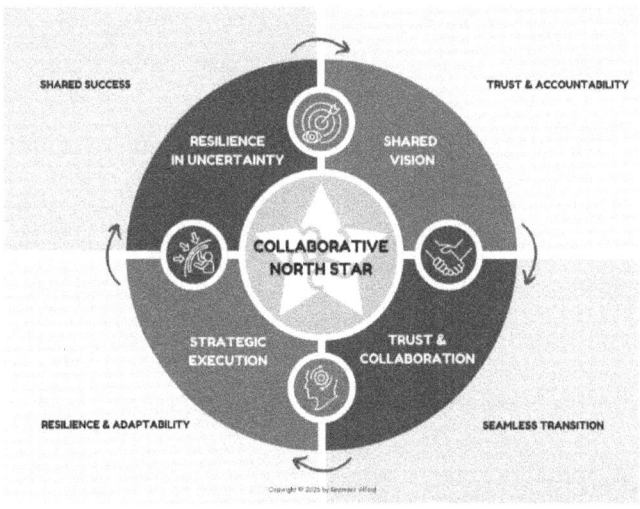

This visual representation illustrates how the framework aligns leadership principles to create a high-functioning, collaborative team.

Each component builds upon the next, creating a **cycle of continuous improvement** that enhances teamwork, adaptability, and long-term success.

Core Foundational Principles of the Framework

1. Establishing a Shared Vision

A strong team starts with a clear direction. Without a shared vision, people focus on individual tasks rather than the collective mission.

Leaders using the **Collaborative North Star Framework** ensure that every team member understands:

- The team's purpose and long-term goals.
- How their role contributes to the bigger picture.
- Why collaboration strengthens overall success.

When leaders reinforce this vision, it becomes more than words—it becomes a **guiding force** that shapes decisions and actions.

2. Building Trust and Collaboration

Trust allows teams to work together without hesitation. It grows through transparency, reliability, and shared experiences. Without trust, people hold back ideas, hesitate to ask for help, and focus more on protecting themselves than contributing to the team's success.

In a high-trust environment, team members:

- Communicate openly and address challenges together.
- Hold themselves and others accountable.

- Feel valued and empowered to contribute their best work.

Leaders must intentionally **foster trust** through **transparency, consistency, and genuine engagement**. Without it, even the best strategies fall apart.

3. Strengthening Leadership Transitions

Change is inevitable. Whether it is a leadership shift, role reassignment, or new initiative, teams succeed when transitions are smooth and well-executed.

4. Resilience in Uncertainty

Leaders and teams who can prepare for changes that impact working relationships are better aligned to accomplish their goals. Amid uncertain times, they find strength to uphold each other.

The **Collaborative North Star Framework** prepares teams for change by ensuring:

- Clear knowledge transfer between outgoing and incoming leaders.
- Defined expectations for new roles and responsibilities.
- Continued momentum, preventing disruptions in progress.

Much like a relay race, successful leadership transitions depend on **effective handoffs**. When teams manage these transitions well, they maintain stability and avoid setbacks.

How This Framework Transforms Leadership

Leaders who implement the **Collaborative North Star Framework** see measurable improvements in team dynamics and performance. The shift from **individual focus to collective success** results in:

- Higher engagement and motivation.
- More efficient teamwork and fewer delays.
- Stronger communication and problem-solving.
- Greater adaptability to change.

Leaders spend less time fixing problems and more time guiding their teams toward meaningful progress. Collaboration becomes second nature, and people feel a deep connection to their work.

Bringing the Framework to Life

Real transformation happens when leadership principles move from theory to practice. The **Collaborative North Star Framework** has helped achieve clarity, efficiency, and resilience in real-world settings.

To demonstrate its impact, I want to share with you an experience of the framework. During a leadership retreat, I had the opportunity to demonstrate the framework in action. One summer afternoon, I gathered my team for a day of strategic discussions and team-building exercises. As part of our activities, we watched a recording of the **2024 Women's Olympic 4x100-meter relay race**, an event that perfectly captured the power of trust, teamwork, and seamless transitions.

Lessons from the Track: A Leadership Relay

What unfolded on the track mirrored the very essence of the Collaborative North Star Framework. It was more than a race—it was a masterclass in leadership, precision, and shared purpose.

I had planned it as a moment of inspiration, yet it turned out to be much more. As we watched Sha'Carri Richardson, Gabby Thomas, Melissa Jefferson, and Teahna "Teetee" Terry take their places, the room was electric with anticipation. I'm sure my leaders were wondering what I was up to, but I knew the symbolism that would soon unfold.

The race conditions were far from ideal; it was raining, and the track glistened with water, creating challenging running conditions. As the race unfolded, I couldn't help to reflect on the parallels of our own experiences. The rain reminded me of the unpredictable challenges we face in leadership, and I pointed this out in our discussion afterward. The competition was fierce, with teams from Jamaica, Great Britain, and Canada pushing hard, much like the pressures we feel from external forces. Yet, the focus and determination of the U.S. team were unwavering, and it was clear that their preparation and trust in one another were the foundation of their success.

Melissa Jefferson began the race with a powerful start. Despite the slick track, her strides were deliberate and strong, setting a steady pace. As she approached the first exchange zone, the baton handoff to Gabby Thomas was executed flawlessly. Thomas maintained their momentum, navigating the curve with skill and precision, all while the rain continued to pour. The tension in the room was palpable as we watched the Jamaican and British teams close in.

The second exchange to Teetee Terry was critical. The baton transfer under such conditions could easily go awry, but Terry's focus and confidence shone through. She surged ahead, her determination cutting through the rain-soaked air. Finally, the baton reached Sha'Carri Richardson, the anchor. Her speed and intensity were nothing short of electrifying. With each stride, she pulled further ahead, leaving their competitors behind. When she crossed the finish line, securing the gold medal for Team USA, the room erupted into cheers. For a moment, it felt like we were there in Paris, sharing in their victory.

After the race, we discussed what we had witnessed, but it was critical to also watch the post-race interview. The athletes' reflections resonated deeply with our team. Richardson's words stuck with me: "It wasn't just about any one of us. It was about all of us working together, trusting each other, and believing in our shared goal. That's what got us here." Thomas added, "The baton handoffs were everything. You can't win a relay without smooth exchanges. We worked hard to get that right, and it showed today." Their emphasis on trust, preparation, and collaboration mirrored the principles of the Collaborative North Star I had been sharing with my team.

It was critical to focus on the types of races to further connect us, as the race became a powerful metaphor for our work. Consider the sprint, for instance—a short, explosive burst of energy that demands focus, speed, and precision. These races are exhilarating but require immense preparation and mental toughness to execute perfectly.

Then there's the marathon, the ultimate test of endurance and pacing. Marathon runners, such as Jesse Owens, must balance strategy with stamina, often pushing their limits to finish strong over grueling long distances.

Finally, we have the dash—a middle-distance race that combines the intensity of a sprint with the strategic pacing of a marathon. Athletes in this category, like the 800-meter specialists, excel by mastering the balance between speed and endurance.

But perhaps the most illustrative metaphor for leadership is the relay race. Unlike the other races, a relay requires seamless teamwork. While other races may focus on individual brilliance, the relay is about how effectively the baton is passed from one runner to the next. Each runner's performance impacts the entire team's success, making trust and collaboration paramount.

The **baton** symbolized our shared vision and goals, and the **handoffs** symbolized the unique contributions of our team members. The rain was a reminder that conditions will not always be favorable, yet with preparation, trust, and determination, success is still possible. Each of us has a role to play, and our ability to work together seamlessly determines the outcome.

The Collaborative North Star Impact

Anchored in four principles: shared vision, trust and collaboration, strategic execution, and resilience in uncertainty we were able to meet and achieve our goals of collaboration, trust, and a shared vision.

Using the relay race as our backdrop for discussion, it was a rewarding leadership moment seeing this concept come to life within my own team. We faced a significant organizational change that many saw as an insurmountable challenge. Drawing on the principles of the *Collaborative North Star*, we reframed the situation—not as a hurdle but as an opportunity to strengthen teamwork and align more closely with our vision. By the end of the day, we achieved our goals and grew closer as a team, with a renewed sense of purpose and determination, while walking away with individual and team commitments to guide our work and relationships.

In this chapter, you've gotten a glimpse of the Collaborative North Star Framework, but there's much more to explore. In my forthcoming book, I'll take you step by step through each pillar and principle, complete with case studies, exercises, and implementation strategies. If you're ready to lead with unwavering confidence, be on the lookout for this deep dive—it's a resource that will equip you for the leadership journey ahead.

Embracing the Leadership Journey

If you haven't realized by now, mistakes are inevitable, but they have an eerie truth – they present opportunities to learn and improve. In that growth period, which never ends, you'll need to have the courage to own your missteps, the humility to learn from them, and the determination to grow.

To you, the aspiring, new, or experienced leader: embrace the power of vision. Define a clear, compelling direction for your team. Communicate it with passion, align it with your values, and let it guide your decisions. Leadership thrives on trust, collaboration, and shared purpose—so build it together.

As you move forward, remember the lessons of the **sprint**, the **marathon**, and the **relay** race. Each presents unique challenges, but all demand focus, resilience, and commitment. Stay the course, play your role with excellence, and pass the baton with care. And when the race is won, celebrate—not as an individual achievement, but as the triumph of a united team.

CHAPTER SEVEN
Inauthentic Leadership

> "Potential is the realization of your proven abilities. When you embrace who you are you unlock things unimaginable."

What can I share with you about being authentic as a leader? Some might say nothing, while others might say a whole lot. Let's explore this together because authenticity—or the lack of it—is something many leaders grapple with early in their careers.

Think about it—*why do people lead the way they do at first?* The answer is simple: they emulate what they see. From the moment we are born, we absorb the world around us, mirroring behaviors, mannerisms, and even speech. One of the most fascinating things in life is how quickly babies pick up habits and language, almost as if they are tiny sponges soaking up every sound and action placed before them.

I was reminded of this the other day while watching a video of a toddler attempting to navigate his way down a small set of stairs. He was determined, his little legs wobbling as he carefully placed one foot in front of the other. But as toddlers often do, he miscalculated a step, lost his balance, and tumbled down. Thankfully, he wasn't hurt. Instead, as he landed with a plop, he immediately popped back up, dusted himself off, and—without hesitation—exclaimed, *"Shit!"*

The moment was both hilarious and telling. His parent, clearly caught off guard but amused, instinctively repeated the word right back to him. And just like that, the toddler proudly echoed, *"Shit!"* again, his little voice ringing with confidence as if he had just mastered a new and important word.

It was a perfect example of how children mimic what they hear and see, often without understanding the meaning behind it. In that brief, comical exchange, it became evident how effortlessly habits and language take root in young minds. They don't just learn from what we intentionally teach them—they learn from everything we do.

For me, and I'm sure for many others, the way we first started leading was much the same. We modeled ourselves after the leaders we encountered over time. Their habits and strategies—both good and bad—became the foundation of our own leadership approach. Initially, this method may work, but over time, it can feel stale and inauthentic if it doesn't truly align with who we are.

Learning from Leadership Styles

Throughout my career, I've worked with many leaders, each bringing a unique style to the table. Some were visionaries, charting new paths with bold ideas. Others excelled at fostering collaboration, making everyone feel heard and valued. Some were meticulous, ensuring no detail was overlooked. And then, there were those who struggled—leaders whose rigidity or lack of connection held them back. As I developed, every encounter taught me something: what to emulate, what to avoid, and how critical it is to adapt your approach to meet the needs of those you lead. Some I admired and learned from, others... well, let's just say their approach taught me exactly what *not* to do. The differences in my respect for them had little to do with their skill or expertise and everything to do with their authenticity.

The 90/10 Rule of Leadership

When I transitioned into higher education from a six year career in the fast food industry, I met Terry Everson, a leadership coach with an uncanny ability to distill complex ideas into lasting wisdom. Terry was a tall, slender-built man, standing about 6'1", with a warm and welcoming personality that instantly put people at ease. His hair—a blend of gray and white—served as a quiet testament to his experience and wisdom. He had a commanding presence, not through intimidation, but through sheer enthusiasm and passion for training.

Every time we crossed paths, he carried a stack of leadership workbooks, always prepared to share insights that could shift perspectives and inspire growth. One day in a training session, he said, *"A leader should operate 90% in personal power and 10% in position power."* At first, I didn't fully grasp it. But as my career unfolded, it clicked.

> Leadership isn't about titles or authority—it's about relationships.

Think about that. Isn't being *"The Boss"* enough to inspire a team? Absolutely not! Positional authority might grant decision-making power, but it doesn't build loyalty or commitment. People follow leaders they trust and respect, not just those with a title. Building that trust requires aligning your actions with your values, demonstrating integrity, and genuinely caring for your team's well-being. Leadership rooted in relationships—not hierarchy—is what truly inspires people to go above and beyond.

The Cost of Inauthenticity

Of course, being authentic as a leader isn't always easy. Authenticity is a buzzword often thrown around but not always understood. According to the *Oxford Dictionary,* being inauthentic means "not made or done in a way that reflects tradition or faithfully resembles an original." That might not sound alarming—until you experience a leader whose lack of authenticity creates disconnection within a team. I know this firsthand because I've been that leader. I've sat in the seat of knowing my team didn't truly understand who I was. And if I'm honest, at the time, I didn't want them to. I built barriers to protect myself from vulnerability, but in doing so, I isolated myself from them.

Looking back, I see how that stance undermined what we could have accomplished together. I wanted to inspire my team and produce great results, but how could I when I wasn't fully invested in showing up as my true self? I was molding myself to meet perceived expectations—a phenomenon I now call "copycat syndrome." It's exhausting, and worse, it's limiting. I had to learn that embracing my authentic self wasn't just about me; it was about creating an environment where my team felt safe to do the same.

A Personal Journey to Authentic Leadership

When I wrote my first book, *Oakland Hills, Milwaukee Rivers,* I shared my journey—from the sun-soaked streets of California to the snow-covered landscapes of Wisconsin—reflecting on my challenges as a young Black boy growing up. It was a story of resilience, triumph, and valuable lessons. But it wasn't just a geographic shift; it was a profound transformation of my identity and worldview.

Writing it meant uncovering deeply personal experiences—some painful, some defining. It was a moment of vulnerability, a decision to open up to the world. I specifically chose to share it with my leadership team to offer them a window into what shaped me and how I lead. That decision became a pivotal and liberating moment. By allowing them to see my authentic self, we connected on a deeper level.

That's the power of authenticity in leadership—it fosters genuine relationships built on trust and understanding. Our relationships evolved in ways I deeply appreciated as we continued our work together.

Why Authenticity Matters in Today's Workplace

In today's world, where cultural competence and psychological safety are more important than ever, authenticity isn't just a nice-to-have—it's a necessity. A 2022 McKinsey & Company report found that employees in inclusive environments are 47% more likely to stay with their organizations and 90% more likely to trust their leadership.[10] This demonstrates that fostering a culture where individuals feel safe to be themselves isn't just good leadership—it's a strategic advantage.

Teams thrive when leaders cultivate environments where authenticity is not only welcomed but encouraged. But how do we get there?

Five Lessons for Leading Authentically

Here are a few lessons I've learned—sometimes the hard way—that may help you on your leadership journey:

1. Develop Self-Awareness

Authenticity starts with knowing yourself. Leaders should regularly reflect on their values, strengths, and weaknesses. I've learned to ask myself tough questions: What do I stand for? What are my blind spots? Self-awareness helps align actions with principles, leading to more genuine interactions.

2. Communicate Transparently

Authentic leaders foster open and honest communication. At the outset of my career, I hesitated to share my thoughts, fearing it might seem unprofessional. But when I embraced transparency—even admitting mistakes—trust within my team grew. When leaders communicate openly, they encourage their teams to do the same, creating a culture of trust and collaboration.

3. Lead by Example

Actions speak louder than words. Read that again for the people in the back—*actions speak louder than words.* I've learned that modeling integrity, accountability, and vulnerability creates a powerful ripple effect.

Once, I made a mistake that significantly impacted my team's workload. Instead of deflecting blame, I owned it. The result? My team respected me more and felt empowered to take accountability themselves. Turns out, admitting you're human isn't a leadership flaw—it's a strength.

4. Embrace Diversity in Leadership

Authenticity looks different for everyone. As leaders, we have the opportunity to celebrate the diverse perspectives and experiences within our teams. Embracing an inclusive and authentic leadership style fosters innovation and strengthens collaboration.

5. Accept the Challenges

Leading authentically isn't always easy. To be blunt—vulnerability can sometimes be mistaken for weakness. I've faced my fair share of skeptical looks when choosing openness, especially in environments that cling to traditional, top-down leadership. But here's the thing: it's worth it.

Authentic leadership builds trust, drives engagement, and keeps people around longer—which is great because hiring is exhausting. In fact, studies show that engaged employees outperform disengaged ones by over 200%, according to a Gallup workplace engagement report.[12] If that's not a reason to embrace authenticity, I don't know what is.

The Transformational Power of Authentic Leadership

So, where does this leave us? It's easy to view authenticity as a "someday" goal—something you'll get to when the timing is right, when you have more experience, or maybe after your next coffee. But here's the truth: authenticity isn't a luxury; it's a game-changer. When you embrace it, you unlock a level of leadership that isn't just effective—it's transformative.

Yes, it requires vulnerability. Yes, it can be uncomfortable. But the rewards—trust, engagement, and resilience—are more than worth it. Think of it like going to the gym for the first time in a while. At first, it's awkward, maybe even painful. You second-guess yourself, wondering if you're using the equipment right or if everyone can tell you have no idea what you're doing. But over time, with consistency, you get stronger, more confident, and the results speak for themselves. Authentic leadership works the same way—the more you lean into it, the stronger your connections and influence become.

Now, take a moment to reflect on your own leadership journey. Grab a notebook (or the back of that receipt in your pocket or purse) and ask yourself:

What's holding me back from being my true self?

How can I create space for my team to do the same?

And most importantly, what steps can I take today to lead authentically—not just for my own growth but for the success of those I lead?

Write down your answers. Let them guide you as you redefine your relationships and create a more genuine leadership experience.

At the end of the day, leadership is all about relationships—and the strongest ones are built on authenticity. My advice? Embrace who you are, lean into your values, and lead in a way that is true, bold, and unapologetically you.

PART THREE: PRIORITIZING THE MATTERS

Every action begins with a thought, and every outcome is anchored in a decision.

CHAPTER EIGHT
TBD

"It's okay not to water things that refuse to grow."

Reading the title of this chapter, I bet you were curious about where I was going with this. If you love deciphering acronyms, you probably assumed I was talking about *"To Be Determined,"* right? Nope, not this time—though, let's be honest, life itself is pretty much one giant *TBD* moment.

In this chapter, I want to talk about something crucial in leadership that many people try to sidestep: **"The Big Decisions."** You know, the ones that keep you up at night, have you pacing the floor, or make you wish there was a magic 8-ball for leadership.

Before we dive in, think about a *TBD moment* in your life—a time when everything hinged on your ability to make a decision. Maybe it was choosing between two job offers, deciding whether to move to a new city, or even just picking a restaurant when everyone in the group said, *"I don't care, you decide."* (Truth be told—that last one can feel just as stressful.)

Hold onto that moment, keep it in your back pocket, because we're going to revisit it later.

For some reason, making high-stakes decisions as a leader in the workplace feels different than in our personal lives. Maybe it's because more is at stake? Maybe it's because more people are involved? Or maybe it's because more people are watching. Either way, decisions have to be made, and you, my friend, are the one who has to make them when the time comes.

The Balancing Act of Leadership

Leadership is an intricate dance between courage and compassion—a balancing act that often demands tough choices to drive progress. Over the years, I've found myself in plenty of *TBD* moments where I had to make decisions about a person, an organizational direction, or sometimes, a test of my own values. These moments are pivotal—often stressful—but undeniably essential for both the organization's success and your growth as a leader.

But, let me be honest for a second: I *hated*—yes, *hated*—being in those situations. I told you I was going to be vulnerable, right? Right.

So, why did I hate it? Well, it mostly came down to this: making a decision meant I had to *own* whatever the outcome was going to be. And, of course, if it was the wrong decision? I probably wouldn't hear the end of it. There's no better way to sit in the residual of a bad decision than realizing you'll be hearing about it at the next company meeting... and possibly in the breakroom for months. People don't let you forget, do they?

Avoidance, though, is just as bad. It's like knowing you should be folding your laundry but instead choosing to binge-watch Netflix for the fourth hour in a row. You *know* you'll regret it later, but you still do it anyway. And guess what? It catches up with you.

When Instincts Are Ignored

Tough decisions don't get easier but avoiding them only makes things worse. One of my most profound lessons came from what should have been a straightforward hiring decision. At the time, my career was advancing, and I needed to delegate responsibilities so I could focus on bigger organizational goals—and, honestly, stop doing three jobs at once. As chair of the hiring committee, I felt the weight of selecting my replacement, knowing this role demanded excellence. The process was rocky from the start, with warning signs I chose to ignore in my haste to fill the position. My gut told me to pause, even fail the search if necessary, but I ignored it.

The result? A nightmare that disrupted my team's cohesion and left some serious scars. While the candidate's qualifications checked every box—seriously, I'm talking a perfect resume—the fit just wasn't there. My failure to trust my instincts didn't just shake up the team—it became a defining lesson in leadership.

Decisions, especially the big ones, must align with your values and the organization's mission. Looking back, I've learned that as a hiring manager, it's okay to deviate from the *"perfect process"* if it means making a decision that might not be immediately popular. In this case, I relied way too much on the committee's consensus and not enough on my own gut feeling. It's like going to a potluck, seeing everyone's fancy dishes, and thinking, *"Well, it must be great because everyone's bringing it."* But then, one bite... and you realize, not all recipes were made equal.

That was my fault, and it was my responsibility to do what I knew was best. Yet, I ignored my instincts, and the aftermath lingered for a while. A mistake I never plan to make again.

The lesson? Trust your gut. It's there for a reason.

Knowing When to Let Go

We as people who are passionate pour time and energy into projects, people, or initiatives hoping they'll eventually succeed. But sometimes, we have to recognize when to let go—or allow something to be planted in someone else's garden where it might actually thrive. Growth requires discernment, and part of that discernment is knowing when to step back. I once wrote a "KeyWORDS" quote that stuck with me: *"It's okay not to water things that refuse to grow."* When this profound thought came to me, it made perfect sense.

> Sometimes, we invest our energy into people, things, or situations that don't produce the outcomes we envisioned. We take on the responsibility of nurturing them—providing water and sunlight—yet we continue to watch them wither. The leaves slowly fade because they were never in the right environment to thrive.

Sounds insane right? It definitely does and unfortunately it happens more too often in our organizations.

Tough Calls That Redefine Leadership

In one of my roles, I had to make the tough call to restructure a department. The inefficiencies had been tolerated for far too long causing fractured teams, missed opportunities for collaboration, and resources going to waste. The restructuring should've happened years ago, but it kept getting delayed because no one wanted to rock the boat. We were all busy pretending the elephant in the room wasn't actually sitting on top of us. But eventually, we had to face the facts:

we weren't being good stewards of our resources, and as a result, we weren't making the impact we could've.

I couldn't just move a few pieces around like a game of Tetris—I had to reset the foundation of our work so the unit could actually thrive. Let's just say, it wasn't exactly a smooth launch. It required tough conversations, transparency, and a level of commitment to the organization's mission.

This shift required me to keep reiterating the *"why"* while also being mindful of the need for change management, remembering that people are our greatest asset (even when some really were not interested in going through the needed steps). The process was far from easy, but the results were transformational. Teams started collaborating, communication improved, and the ripple effect was so noticeable to those around.

That experience reinforced a critical lesson: even when decisions are uncomfortable, delaying them only creates bigger headaches down the road. It reminded me of Jim Collins' book *Good to Great*, where he emphasized that getting people in the right seats on the bus is crucial for success. Our realignment was necessary to ensure we could make a real impact in the future.

Let's picture this: A school bus full of 20 kids, fresh off a museum field trip, breaks down on the side of the road. Onboard, there's a bus driver, a mechanic, and a chaperone.

Now, instead of troubleshooting or calling for help, the bus driver sits on the steps, overwhelmed, saying, "I don't know anything about engines."

The mechanic, who could easily fix the issue, takes charge of managing the kids. "Alright, everyone, let's stay calm!" he shouts, trying to line them up in an orderly fashion. But his impatience and lack of authority only make things worse—the kids laugh, ignore him, and a few start jumping on the seats.

Meanwhile, the chaperone, who is usually great with kids, rolls up her sleeves and heads to the engine, convinced she can fix it. But when she sees a snapped belt and smoke rising from the radiator, she quickly realizes she has no clue what she's doing.

In this moment, none of them are in their element. The bus driver's not driving, the mechanic's not fixing, and the chaperone's not chaperoning.

This is where leadership kicks in. Someone has to admit they're not being effective and make the tough decision to step up. The bus driver shouldn't be sitting on the steps, the chaperone shouldn't be under the hood, and the mechanic shouldn't be trying to calm the kids. When everyone's focused on the wrong task, the bus stays stuck—or in my case, the situation remains stuck.

I share this story because a strong leader doesn't step up to do everything—they step up to ensure the right people are doing what they do best. Only then can real progress happen.

A Framework for Decision-Making

When facing tough calls, I've developed a personal framework for making decisions.

Clarify the core problem. What really needs to change, and why? The real issue is often deeper than what's on the surface. For example, in the restructuring, the real problem wasn't just inefficiency—it was a culture resistant to accountability.

Evaluate potential outcomes through the lens of organizational values and long-term goals. How does this decision align with our mission? Thinking long-term helps anchor decisions and brings clarity to the process.

Seek diverse perspectives. Trusted colleagues and key stakeholders can offer insights I might have missed. During the restructuring, I consulted team members individually to design a plan that minimized disruptions while achieving the necessary changes. Having sounding boards doesn't mean you lack confidence—it means you're making an informed decision. It's like proofreading a paper. Your brain knows what you meant to write, but sometimes your fingers don't capture the thought correctly. Another set of eyes can catch what you missed.

Commit to decisive action. Once a decision is made, hesitation only breeds uncertainty. Communicate decisions clearly and stick to them. And trust me, people will always have opinions. Some will want to pull you off track, creating exceptions and loopholes. Leadership won't make everyone happy but make the right choices and stand by them – *unshaken*.

Leadership in Crisis

Alright, do you still have that piece of paper I asked you to tuck away? Well, it's time to pull it out because TBD you made had an audience that we'll illuminate here. As we lean into this section, think about who was watching or waiting on you to make the decision. What did they mean to you? Did their thoughts of you have any bearing of what you ultimately decided? If so, why is that? Think about that.

Does our decisions carry the weight of someone's opinion of us or are we okay with making the decision regardless of opinions?

For this next piece of leadership advice, I want you to center yourself and read these words very carefully - *people are always watching*. It is like you are on public display. Your team isn't just observing what decisions you make but how you make them. In the early stages of my professional journey, I faced a crisis where my team looked to me for guidance. That moment taught me that leadership is about how you navigate uncertainty with integrity and not just about the outcome.

The pandemic was a prime example. Every decision was scrutinized, emotions were high, and uncertainty was constant. Leaders had to balance Centers for Disease Control and Prevention (CDC) guidelines, government regulations, and staff well-being. Every cough got a suspicious glance, and every sniffle raised alarm bells. Decisions had to be firm and well-articulated. Some leaders wavered, trying to accommodate every concern, but I learned that too much flexibility in big decisions leads to chaos. If your reputation says anything, let it be that you're decisive, not that you struggle to make a call.

The Residual Plan

One mistake leaders make is assuming the job is done after TBD's. That's where a residual plan comes in—addressing what happens before, during, and after the decision. Here are a few strategies to consider avoiding rocky situations.

Prioritize Follow-Through

Your decisions will have a ripple effect, and if you don't plan for it, things can quickly get out of control. A delay or inconsistency can erode trust within your team. Think of it like building a house: if the foundation is shaky, the entire structure will eventually collapse.

Strategy: Set clear timelines and communicate regularly about progress. For example, if you're implementing a new software system, break it down into manageable steps with deadlines. Keep everyone updated, even if there are delays, so people know you're on top of things.

Support Those Affected

Whether through training, resources, or simply being available, it's essential to have a strategy in place to support those impacted by the change. Think of it like a coach preparing their team for a big game—everyone needs the right tools to succeed.

Strategy: Offer ongoing training and check-ins. For instance, if you're restructuring a team like I did, provide regular touch bases and guidance during the transition period. This helps people feel supported and less anxious about the change.

Monitor Outcomes

A decision isn't truly complete until you've assessed its impact and made adjustments as needed. It's like adjusting your route when you hit traffic—if you're like me, you don't just sit there, you find a way to get around it and keep moving forward.

Strategy: Regularly assess key metrics and seek input from those directly affected. For example, after launching a new process improvement, track feedback and adjust processes if necessary. This ensures you're staying on track.

Reflect on the Process

Seeking feedback helps refine your approach for future decisions. Think of it like reviewing game footage—you learn from what went well and what could be improved. If I'm honest, we sometimes do a horrible job at this because we always want to hear the good when the bad is just as impactful.

Strategy: After the decision has been made and the results are in, gather feedback from your team and stakeholders. For example, if you've rolled out a new policy, ask for anonymous feedback about what worked and what didn't. Use this to tweak your approach next time.

Through trial and error, these strategies have helped me as a leader. I hope they will help you as well to make decisions that not only address immediate needs but also create a more resilient, trusting, and effective team in the long run. When you prioritize follow-through, support those affected, monitor outcomes, and reflect on the process, you'll find yourself making smarter, more impactful decisions that save you time and energy later. Lessons I didn't know in the beginning.

The Reality of Leadership

Now what do you do when you make a decision and it's not favorable? Do you back away from the table or do you continue to move forward? My answer? It depends.

You must first acknowledge that not every decision will be celebrated. If you thought it would be, let me shake you to wake you up from that fairy tale. Some will challenge you, and others will question your choices. But your job isn't to please everyone—it's to lead with integrity and purpose. The truth is leadership is like walking a tightrope. You balance the needs of the organization with the well-being of your team while staying true to your principles. In higher education (or any organization for that matter), the stakes are deeply personal. Your decisions impact people, not just spreadsheets. Recognizing that responsibility makes leadership both challenging and incredibly rewarding. If your decision was made for the right reason, then stay at the table. However, if it was done for the wrong one, then you will eventually encounter problems. You will have to take the responsibility to address the situation to change directions. It's all apart of the learning experience.

Looking back, I appreciate the lessons from both my missteps and my successes. Each decision, good or bad, has shaped me. That's why I remind myself of the opening KeyWORDS quote: *"It's okay not to water things that refuse to grow."* Some things need to be let go. And that's okay.

To you, my advice is simple: *don't shy away from tough decisions.* Your team isn't watching to scrutinize you—they're looking to see how they can follow your lead. Show them that leadership is about courage, compassion, and an unwavering commitment to the mission. The journey isn't easy, but it's worth every step.

CHAPTER NINE
A Balancing Act

> "At some point, centering becomes a choice.
> You can accept it to catapult forward
> or deny it and catapult backward."

It was December 2016, and I was thrilled about the opportunity to step into a leadership role and prove what I was capable of achieving. At that time, my life was in a phase of significant transition—I was a single man with no kids, nearing the finish line of my doctoral degree, and ready to take on new challenges. The holiday season gave me a moment to unwind from my current job and mentally prepare for what lay ahead. Excitement filled the air, but it was laced with apprehension. I was stepping into an environment that had experienced instability in leadership for the past three to four years. The task awaiting me wasn't just daunting; it was colossal.

A thirty-three-page peer-reviewed assessment laid before me, outlining the organization's issues. This document wasn't just a to-do list—it was a documented report of everything that could go wrong if left unaddressed. Wanting to be as prepared as possible, I requested all the information I could gather before my official start date to gain a fair understanding of what I was walking into. But before diving into what felt like a mountain of challenges, I took a step back to decompress. Humor became my sanctuary, and I turned to an unlikely source of inspiration: a movie I had heard about from friends but never watched, *The Devil Wears Prada*.

This film had been out for years and was already a classic for fashion lovers and anyone intrigued by the dynamics of workplace culture. At its core, the movie is about a young journalist, Andy Sachs (played by Anne Hathaway), who lands a job as an assistant to the powerful, impeccably dressed, and often terrifying editor-in-chief of *Runway* magazine, Miranda Priestly (played by Meryl Streep). Miranda is the epitome of influence and authority, wielding her power with precision and control over everyone around her.

Other notable characters include Emily Charlton (Emily Blunt), Miranda's first assistant, who takes great pride in her position but struggles with her health and overwork, and Nigel Kipling (Stanley Tucci), a warm yet brutally honest creative director who mentors Andy. Together, they create a world of sharp contrasts: immense glamour weaved with high stakes and emotional tolls.

The Devil Wears Prada explores themes that transcend fashion, offering lessons on leadership, influence, and the importance of balancing professional and personal life. As I watched, I couldn't help but find parallels between the story and my upcoming role. The movie showcased Miranda's meticulous power, her unrelenting standards, and the ripple affects her leadership style had on those around her. Her control extended far beyond assigning tasks—it shaped the very culture of the organization.

Watching the movie, I couldn't help but imagine myself as a male "Miranda." Would someone fetch my coffee each morning or hang up my coat? Would my calls be scheduled seamlessly without my involvement? The fantasy was entertaining but fleeting because, deep down, I knew my personality didn't align with that level of rigidity. The movie's lessons on the power of influence and organizational dynamics left a lasting impression, though.

What stood out most was the movie's commentary on work-life balance—or the lack thereof. Miranda's team rarely had a moment to themselves, and interruptions frequently sabotaged their personal lives. The culture depicted in the movie was one of constant availability, which eroded relationships and well-being. It wasn't just about staying late to finish a project; it was about control. That struck a chord with me. While leadership requires dedication and extra effort at times, there must be boundaries. The absence of balance shown in the film served as a cautionary tale for me as I prepared to lead my department.

By the time the credits rolled, I felt both entertained and reflective. *The Devil Wears Prada* didn't just make me laugh but it gave me a lens through which to view my new role. It was a reminder of what I wanted to avoid as a leader and what I wanted to embrace: authenticity, influence, and the ability to inspire without overwhelming. As I entered that next chapter of my career, I was determined to lead with intentionality—balancing the drive for excellence with the humanity that fosters both growth and respect. Unfortunately, when I stepped foot on the campus, those lessons that were so clear to me in the movie went out the window and I began to sink into a work ethic that claimed all of my time relentlessly without any remorse because I allowed it.

The Cost of Overcommitment

My first year was hard – extremely hard if I am honest. The work was overwhelming and the dynamics within the office were apparent. People were nice to me for the most part, but there was always this notion in the back of people's minds wondering how long I would last. On one occasion someone said to me, "We wonder how long you're going to be around." That was an eye-opening moment as it demonstrated the confidence that had been left with leadership within the department. Yet, it was a battle I was willing to fight and one I took on with a great amount of sacrifice.

As a leader—whether new to a profession or a role—it's crucial to maintain balance. One mistake I made early on was physically exhausting myself by working 60-70 hours a week, thinking it was the only way to get things done. I felt the demand was so great that I needed to invest all my time in resolving problems and clearing them off my list. What I didn't realize at the time was that work will always be there, but the opportunity to create and build memories with family and friends is short. The pressure I put on myself silently began to affect my health, but I didn't recognize it. While others might have seen my work ethic as admirable, it set an unintended tone—suggesting that working overtime and long hours was the norm. Unfortunately, at that point, I didn't have anyone in my ear reminding me otherwise.

The Hidden Truths in Leadership

In my eyes, I had something to prove. It wasn't just my first year; I was also a Black man—*the* first one in the role. The pressure to set an example for the culture was undeniable. We often don't talk about the context of leadership roles in professional settings—especially for people of color. The reality is that we are held to higher expectations than our counterparts. When we fail, we're often generalized, as if our mistakes reflect the whole race. So, we find ourselves working twice as hard, not just to prove ourselves, but to prove that we are just as capable and qualified as anyone else. A 2019 Korn Ferry study found that 57% of Black leaders in corporate America said they had to work *twice as hard* and accomplish *twice as much* as their peers just to be seen as equals.[11] It's a harsh reality, but it's the daily struggle many people of color face.

As I reflected on the importance of balance in leadership—a lesson that every leader, new or experienced, should take to heart—I realized there are several key takeaways to consider. These lessons can help you protect your well-being, support your family, and safeguard your mental health throughout your leadership journey.

Unveiling Boundaries of Unsung Heroes in Leadership.

Balance – I've mentioned it before, but it's worth emphasizing just how critical it is. Over time, I've learned (often the hard way) that finding the right balance between work and personal life is one of the most essential things a leader can do. It's easy to get swept up in the fast pace of your work, but without balance, even the most passionate leaders can quickly burn out. As a foundation of effective leadership, balance is more than just taking a break. It allows you to maintain your energy, stay focused, and lead with clarity and purpose.

I've seen firsthand how prioritizing holistic well-being can make a real difference. When I started incorporating small, mindful routines into my day—like meditating, reading a daily prayer, or listening to a podcast on my drive to work—my stress levels dropped. Sharing this with others, I realized it set a powerful example, showing that self-care isn't just acceptable—it's essential. Those simple moments became my resets, helping me approach challenges with a fresh perspective and renewed focus.

Drawing a Line in the Sand

As previously shared, there have been times when I thought overcommitting to work would make me feel more dedicated. Oh, did I learn this lesson the hard way! Turns out, working late nights and sacrificing weekends wasn't the magic solution I thought it was—though, at the time, it sure seemed like the noble, 'leaderly' thing to do. I quickly realized that short-term wins could lead to long-term losses.

> Learning when to draw a line in the sand to protect yourself might be the very thing that saves you from unnecessary stress. Boundaries are essential.

I've seen colleagues push themselves too hard, only to lose their sharpness, patience, and even their sense of purpose. And of course, fatigue and stress have a way of creeping in quietly, but their effects are impossible to ignore. Yet, I will admit, it can sometimes be hard to do.

Stories of Always 'Available'

The harsh truth is that sometimes, you have to make sure others know your boundaries. It could be a conversation to clarify that you're not available before or after certain hours, or that you won't be responding to emails at specific times. Before I established those boundaries, there were two occasions when I was contacted by my supervisor while on vacation—my time to reset.

One spring, I found myself in Sorrento, Italy—a place that seemed like it had jumped straight out of a postcard. Picture this: the sun shining brightly from a cloudless sky, the temperature hovering at a perfect 75 degrees. You are strolling along cobblestone streets, passing pastel-colored buildings, with stunning cliffside views overlooking endless turquoise waters. That was me, fully immersed in the magic of vacation, savoring every moment—until my phone rang.

It was my job calling. It had to be an emergency, right? After all, I was on vacation. I picked up, expecting to hear some urgent news. But no—on the other end of the line was my boss, asking for some data about a program I was responsible for. We talked for about 5 to 10 minutes, and then he casually mentioned it was for a report due the following week—and he was just getting a head start on it.

An urgent matter? Hardly. It could have easily waited until I returned in just a few days – but I had not established my boundaries.

Another time, I was in Cartagena, Colombia, speeding across the sea in a boat that bounced relentlessly over the waves. Some friends and I were heading to a private island, a secluded paradise just thirty minutes from shore. The sun glistened on the water, the mist of saltwater splashing on my face and head, and my friends and I were lost in laughter, soaking in the beauty of the moment.

But then—my phone buzzed.

I had been capturing the scenery, wanting to preserve the memory, but instead, I was met with a string of text messages from my supervisor. They knew I was on vacation, yet here I was, fielding work concerns in the middle of the Caribbean Sea.

Those moments—both in Cartagena and Sorrento—left me with a sobering realization: I was never truly off. And that changed everything. From that point on, I recognized the importance of setting firm boundaries intentionally and unapologetically.

When I returned from vacation, my supervisor wanted to catch up about my time away, and that's when I had to share how it felt to be interrupted while I was trying to disconnect. It was a difficult conversation to have, but a necessary one.

Once I set boundaries and genuinely committed to maintaining balance, I found myself showing up as my best self, consistently. That's the advice I leave with you.

The Costs of Ignoring Balance

Now, you might take what I've shared to heart, or, like many of us, you might ignore it. But I'd be doing you a disservice if I didn't also tell you the consequences of ignoring balance—they're very real. I remember working under a leader who was clearly burned out. Their exhaustion and cynicism didn't just affect their mood—it dragged the whole team down. Creativity dwindled, communication faltered, and morale hit rock bottom. It was a harsh reminder of just how crucial it is to protect not only my own energy but also the energy of those I lead.

Relationships

There's another cost to imbalance that often hits closer to home: *relationships*. I've had seasons where I prioritized work so much that personal relationships fell to the side. Those were some of the loneliest moments of my life, and I could feel the strain spilling into my work. A leader who neglects their connections with family, friends, or colleagues isn't just losing out personally—they're also losing the trust and support of the people they need most.

Health

And then there's the impact on health. Chronic stress doesn't just affect your mind—it has real, physical consequences, including anxiety, depression, and even illness. Many driven leaders have had to step back from their careers because they ignored their well-being. People without work-life balance are nearly three times more likely to feel disconnected at work. In fact, 51% of U.S. employees who struggle with balancing work and home life say their job negatively affects their mental health.[13] Watching this unfold around me, I came to a sobering realization: *no job is worth sacrificing your health*. And for me, that lesson came in the form of a heart attack.

My situation was a direct reflection of the stress I carried without any outlet to release it. I pushed myself too hard, and my body made me face the consequences. The reality hit hard—*slow down, pay attention, and take care of yourself if you want to stick around longer.* When it happened, my team was supportive, but I stayed stubborn. There was just so much work to do. I even had a second heart attack and found myself responding to emails and holding virtual meetings from my bed after a procedure. It was a foolish decision on my part, especially when I was telling my staff to take care of themselves.

In that moment, I understood why I did it, but the reason wasn't significant enough to justify it. People recognize that we're all human, and sometimes life forces us to step away in order to become a better version of ourselves. This isn't a path I recommend to anyone, and it's a big part of why I'm sharing this chapter. Learn from my mistakes so you don't have to make the same ones I did. Are you listening to me? I really hope so.

Being Intentional for Balance

For those of us in leadership, balance isn't a luxury—it's a necessity. It's what keeps us resilient, sharp, and capable of inspiring others, all while grounding us when the pressure is high, and the stakes are even higher. If I've learned anything, it's that balance doesn't just happen—you have to fight for it. It requires a conscious choice to prioritize your well-being, pace yourself, and nurture your relationships.

Of course, it's not always easy, but it's always worth it. So, ask yourself: How will you find your balance? How will you lead with strength and purpose? Because when you do, you're not just leading—you're thriving.

While you ponder those questions, let me reiterate a few lessons—because finding balance requires intentionality and a willingness to prioritize what truly matters. Here are few things I've learned.

Setting boundaries between work and personal life is non-negotiable

Establishing specific work hours and protecting personal time for family, hobbies, and self-care creates a healthier rhythm. And yes, sometimes that means putting your foot down with a hard cut-off time and actually sticking to it.

Personally, I try not to work weekends—yes, even when there are things that want my attention. There's just a level of balance I need to maintain. It's not always easy but being clear about what you will and won't do after hours allows you to recharge and be more present in both your personal and professional life. A small step, but trust me, it makes a major difference in how you feel and perform.

Delegating tasks and empowering your team

Another game-changer. When I finally learned to trust others with responsibilities, not only did it lighten my load, but it also gave my team the confidence and space to grow. It's a win-win. Now, I'll admit, though, that wasn't always the case. I was once sucked into the web of "*it won't be done the way I want it.*" And trust me, that web is sticky. I quickly had to learn that there's more than one way to get things done. A control issue? Maybe. But it's one I had to confront in order to support my own well-being. I'm much better now. It's my truth.

Make Time for Personal Well-being

Let's talk about scheduling actual downtime. Take your lunch break—yes, step away from the desk! Read an awesome book (like this one on self-improvement), take a walk, meditate, or dive into a hobby. These intentional moments to recharge make a huge difference in how you lead and show up daily. Balance doesn't just happen—you have to build it, one mindful choice at a time.

And now, picture me holding a giant sign that says *"News Flash"* because this next part is important: As leaders, we set the tone for our environments. Our actions speak louder than words. When we prioritize balance, we send a clear message to our teams that well-being matters.

Thrive, Don't Just Survive

So, as your written mentor, I urge you to reflect regularly on how you manage your time and energy. Life is constantly shifting, and what worked yesterday might not work tomorrow. I've found that stepping back to evaluate where I'm spending my time helps me realign with my values and goals, ensuring that both my work and personal life get the attention they deserve. No sugarcoating it—balance won't look the same for everyone or at every stage of life, but being adaptable is key to sustaining success.

I charge you to not forget about yourself. You can't pour from an empty pitcher, and you certainly can't lead at your best if you're running on fumes. Learn to appreciate the journey, not just the destination. Whether if it's sticking to that fitness routine you swore you'd commit to this year or finally wrapping up a tough project, these moments reinforce why balance matters. They remind us that success and well-being go hand in hand. I'm rooting for you!

CHAPTER TEN
Taking Ownership of YOU

> "I may not be the best, but
> I am the best person to fulfill my destiny."

Here comes that *"News Flash"* sign again—because if we're honest, leadership can be hard at times and you may, along the way, question your own impact. And, you *will* also encounter people who truly don't really care about you. They won't care about:

You as person.

You as an individual.

You as a human being.

It will only be about what you can produce for them. You know what? That's perfectly fine as long as you recognize it early. Those moments—though uncomfortable—can be powerful catalysts for growth and clarity.

This is where self-investment becomes non-negotiable. Knowing *who you are* and leading with confidence will determine the impact you have. Leadership isn't one-size-fits-all; different leaders get different results based on their unique strengths, values, and approach. A quote that inspired this chapter is: *"I may not be the best, but I am the best person to fulfill my destiny."* It serves as a reminder not to fall into the trap of comparison but also centering on who you are and what you seek to accomplish in life. As an individual, your experience, perspective, and leadership style brings something distinct to the table—embrace that. While confidence is key, so is continuous self-investment. If you want optimal results, you must be intentional about becoming the best version of yourself.

Turning Resistance into Fuel

On your journey, learning to transform resistance into fuel—using challenges to refine your skills and elevate your drive—becomes critical for success. It's the classic *"When life gives you lemons, make lemonade"* scenario. Except in leadership, the lemons are sometimes thrown at your head when you least expect it. Still, you take them, make something better, and keep going. It pushes you to rise above the noise with purpose and resilience while demanding a relentless commitment to your worth, your impact, and, most importantly, your destiny.

When I first stepped into leadership, I constantly second-guessed myself. Not because I lacked knowledge, but because I wanted to please everyone.

I quickly learned that leadership isn't about being a people-pleaser; it's about making the right decisions, not just the popular ones. And no matter what you do, someone will always have an opinion.

Take social media, for example. I've posted what I thought were inspiring messages only to receive comments from people who didn't agree—or just wanted to be negative. Content creators always say,

"Don't read the comments," and I should've taken that advice. But even outside of social media, I've seen it in my professional life. As a policy trainer, I spent hours researching, writing, and delivering relatable content, only to have some people critique *my voice* or say they'd rather hear from another trainer. Did it sting? Sure. But was I going to let that shake my confidence? No. If you allow external opinions to define your purpose, you're giving away power that belongs to *you*.

For new leaders—and even experienced ones—it's crucial to stay focused on why you're here and what you were *hired* to do.

The Workforce Has Changed - Have You?

In conversations with professionals across the country, one thing has become clear: today's workforce is focused on transferable skills and career mobility. According to the U.S. Bureau of Labor Statistics, the average employee tenure is now just 3.9 years as of 2024—a stark contrast to the 20 or 30-year careers of previous generations.[14] This shift means organizations have less time to develop and retain talent, and individuals must take personal responsibility for their growth. Leaders who fail to invest in themselves risk stagnation, and in a fast-moving world, stagnation is career kryptonite.

The key? *Avoid comfortability.* Growth doesn't happen when you're coasting—it happens in those uncomfortable moments when you're forced to adapt and improve. Picture this: You're leading a high-pressure project where every decision is under scrutiny. Team dynamics, tight deadlines, expectations—it's all on your shoulders. In those moments, your preparation, mentorship, and self-investment become your strongest assets.

Just like reading this book—you're already gaining insights that will elevate your leadership. Learning from both successes and failures sharpens your ability to navigate challenges with confidence.

The Lifelong Learning Mindset

To lead effectively, you have to think beyond your current role and strategically position yourself for future opportunities. In an article I read that 87% of employees worldwide believe learning and development are essential for career advancement.[15] How are you making sure you're in that number? Are you exposing yourself to new challenges that will expand your skill set? Are you actively seeking knowledge that will position you for long-term success? Career growth and personal development, in 2023, was one of the top 10 focus areas amongst employees,[16] and I don't believe it is changing anytime soon.

Building a Leadership Legacy

Why am I sharing this information with you? Well, it's to amplify that leadership isn't just about holding a title—it's about leaving a legacy. There should be a moment where you build momentum that not only carries *you* forward but also propels those around you. That's the kind of leadership that lasts.

Let's take this conversation up a notch. A core aspect of leadership is leaving a place better than you found it. Ask yourself: *"What will my legacy be?"* Will it be a process you revolutionized to improve efficiency? A program you built that expanded access to critical resources. Or perhaps a cultural shift that allowed people to truly thrive? Any of these is a worthy goal as you move forward in your leadership journey.

I'll be honest—this wasn't something I focused on during my first years in the field. And that was a mistake. A big one. I later realized that prioritizing the legacy you leave behind is one of the most valuable aspects of leadership. In fact, it becomes your professional *bragging rights*. When you walk into a future interview, you can confidently say, "*This was the problem, and this is how I helped solve it.*"

Sure, we all want to do a *good job*. But ask yourself—does that mean maintaining the status quo or transforming it? That's something to reflect on. After all, we can execute the *wrong* thing flawlessly, but can we do the *right* thing just as well?

This is exactly why I emphasize the need to invest in yourself. Growth isn't optional; it's essential. The only way to ensure you become a better, wiser, stronger leader is to commit to self-development. And in today's professional landscape, that's never been more important.

Consider this: 74% of employees believe they lack the necessary skills to succeed in their roles,[17] and according to the World Economic Forum, 44% of workers will need upskilling or reskilling by 2030 just to keep pace with industry demands.[18] Leadership requires adaptability and a willingness to stay ahead of the curve. The moment you stop learning, you start falling behind.

Take a moment to reflect on a time in your career when you implemented change—maybe you streamlined a process, launched a new initiative, or helped shift your organization's culture. What was the impact? Perhaps your workflow overhaul saved countless hours, allowing your team to focus on meaningful work. Or maybe you spearheaded a diversity and inclusion program that gave a voice to those who had been overlooked. These aren't just accomplishments—they're the seeds of a legacy that will continue to grow long after you move on.

As you read this book, my goal is simple: *I want you to thrive*. Thriving in today's fast-changing environment requires one key focus—*self-investment*. Why? Because as you grow, you enable others to grow alongside you.

> Holding a leadership title comes with weighty responsibilities—authority, yes, but also impact. How you invest in yourself to become the best version of you will make all the difference.

By committing to continuous growth, emotional awareness, and self-reflection, leaders can create opportunities—not just for themselves but for those around them—shaping a brighter future for everyone.

Imagine stepping into a new role, brimming with excitement but shadowed by uncertainty. The pressure to succeed is heavy, and expectations loom large. The real question is: How do you ensure this role isn't just another step in your career but a defining moment that propels you forward? The answer? Success starts with the willingness to keep learning.

Leaders who embrace learning maintain their edge in a fast-moving world. Whether it's attending a workshop, taking an online course, or engaging in deep conversations with a mentor, growth opportunities are everywhere. Picture yourself in a room full of professionals, exchanging ideas, walking away with new strategies to help your team thrive. I've learned that we will never have all the answers—and there's power in that realization. Why? Because it keeps your confidence in check. We've all encountered people who act as if they know everything, only to discover they know nothing at all. It's a façade—one built on pride, and pride can lead to your downfall. The best leaders stay curious, seek input from others, and continuously adapt to new challenges.

Understand the people you lead and create an environment where others feel seen, heard, and valued. Emotional intelligence plays a crucial role here. Studies show that leaders with high emotional intelligence are more adaptable, better communicators, and skilled at resolving conflicts with their teams,[19] which speaks volumes about its importance in effective leadership. Picture a team member struggling under a demanding workload. A great leader recognizes the stress, steps in with empathy, and offers support. This kind of awareness builds trust, loyalty, and motivation, fostering a culture where everyone is empowered to do their best work. I've done this time and time again as a servant leader, not just because it's the right thing to do, but because it sets the precedent that we're in this together. When one of us succeeds, we all succeed. I believe there are a few tangible things you should consider when focusing on self-development, and I'd like to share them with you.

Advice to Leaders
Lead yourself first before leading others

Hold yourself accountable for both what you do and what you don't do. Taking time to pause and reflect on your actions is one of the most valuable habits you can develop. Of course, accountability looks different for everyone. But if you're honest and fair with yourself, managing it becomes second nature. We, as leaders, know what's realistically achievable and what's not. It requires discipline and the ability to set boundaries—because truthfully, you can't say yes to everything that lands on your desk, appears in an email, or gets casually mentioned over lunch. Ambition is great, but realism keeps you from drowning. The best leaders ask themselves constantly, 'What am I doing today to make a difference tomorrow?' They focus on creating opportunities, building relationships, and leaving every place better than they found it.

Don't chase perfection—chase progress

I've seen perfectionism stall projects, delay initiatives, and drain the energy out of great ideas. Yes, leaders should strive for excellence but understanding that a margin of error will always exist—and being okay with that—is what truly matters. That margin of error is where we learn, adjust, and improve. If I had never made mistakes along my leadership journey, I wouldn't be writing this book for you now. And guess what? I'll make more mistakes in the future, and that's fine. We learn, we grow, and we do better next time.

As you reflect on these insights, I want you to walk away with five key elements that will influence your approach to self-improvement and help you make it a priority in your life.

Self-Improvement Key Principles

- **People are replaceable, but value is not.** The position you hold today can be filled by someone else tomorrow. What truly matters is the unique value you bring.
- **Diversify your skills—inside and outside your role.** The more versatile you are, the more irreplaceable you become.
- **Build your personal brand.** Your reputation is your currency. Invest in it wisely.
- **Embrace lifelong learning.** Industries evolve. Leaders who keep learning, stay leading.

- **Prioritize your well-being.** You can't pour from an empty cup. Taking care of yourself isn't selfish—it's strategic.
- **Stay future-focused.** The best leaders aren't just thinking about today; they're preparing for what's next.

Each one carries its own weight, but together, they'll guide you toward prioritizing yourself—both personally and professionally.

Reflection Moments for Leaders

I want to challenge you to consider a series of reflection points that will, I believe, make logical sense either now or in the future.

Every experience, challenge, and lesson you encounter shapes the leader you become. I've been on this road long enough to know that while titles change, the impact you leave behind doesn't. It's like a ripple in water—your skills, mindset, and leadership will continue influencing others long after you've moved on. But reaching that point requires intention and a commitment to growth.

I'll admit, it took me a while to realize this. In the beginning, when people left roles under my leadership, I took it personally. I wondered if I could have done more to make them stay. But with time, I saw that organizations don't collapse due to turnover—they thrive because of the value people bring while they're there. My job wasn't to hold on to people who were ready to leave; it was to support their transitions while ensuring the organization remained strong.

Go Beyond Your Job Description

I once worked with someone who refused to take on any task that wasn't explicitly listed in their job responsibilities. At first, I didn't think much of it—until challenges arose and their rigid mindset slowed everything down. It's like driving a car and getting a flat tire but refusing to change it because "that's not my job." You might be great at driving, but that lack of preparation will leave you stranded.

The best leaders expand their skill set beyond what's required. They learn about budgeting, stakeholder engagement, and emerging technologies—not because they have to, but because they *know* it will make them more effective. Every time I stepped outside my comfort zone—whether it was mastering marketing concepts or learning data systems—it strengthened my ability to lead.

Speak Up and Own Your Voice

In the past, I sat in meetings, intimidated by more experienced leaders. Even when I had valuable insights, I often stayed silent. But what's the point of having a seat at the table if you don't *use your voice*? The moment I started contributing, asking questions, and engaging in discussions, people began seeing me not just as someone who was *present*, but as someone who *mattered*.

If you struggle with this, start small—join conversations, attend networking events, and make your voice heard in meetings. Your contributions matter. And the more you engage, the more value you bring.

Take Care of Yourself—Seriously

I grew up hearing people say, *"You're burning the match from both ends,"* but I didn't fully grasp it until I literally burned myself out – pun intended. That was a hard lesson. You matter. And no matter how ambitious you are, you have to protect your well-being. I'm not saying don't give your all to your role—I'm saying don't give so much that you lose yourself in the process. Companies can replace positions overnight, but they *can't* replace *you*. That's why self-care isn't a luxury—it's a necessity.

For me, that meant prioritizing things that brought me joy—traveling, spending time with friends, going to concerts, and embracing the outdoors. Find what refuels you and make it a priority. A healthy, energized leader is a more effective leader.

Stay Future-Focused

Industries evolve, and the skills that matter today won't necessarily matter tomorrow. That's why I make it a point to explore new trends every year—whether it's artificial intelligence, hybrid work models, or sustainability practices. Staying ahead keeps me agile, relevant, and ready for whatever comes next.

But what does it truly mean to be **future-focused**? It's more than just staying informed—it's about actively anticipating change, adapting before it's necessary, and positioning yourself as a leader who **drives innovation rather than reacts to disruption.** Future-focused leadership is the ability to see beyond what's directly in front of you and understand how shifts in technology, industry practices, and societal expectations will shape the way we work. It's about ensuring that the decisions you make today **set you up for success tomorrow.**

A Blockbuster Moment

A friend and I were reminiscing about the days when renting movies at **Blockbuster** was a weekend tradition. We'd pile into the car, browse the shelves, and carefully pick out the latest movie we didn't get to see in the theaters. We laughed about the disappointment of arriving late and finding all the copies gone. Then we asked, *"Whatever happened to Blockbuster?"*

Being curious, I did what many of us do now – I looked to Google. It was then that I found out a simple answer: Blockbuster failed to look ahead.

Blockbuster had the chance to embrace streaming but dismissed **Netflix** as a fad. They had the resources to pivot but clung to what was familiar while the world moved forward. By the time they realized their mistake, it was too late.

It wasn't just Blockbuster, though. **Kodak** invented the first digital camera but resisted the shift from film. Even **Myspace**, who at one point, dominated social media, failed to evolve while Facebook refined its platform.

The lesson? If you're not thinking ahead, you're already falling behind.

This applies to you. If you're developing yourself the same way you did five years ago, without adapting to changes in technology, workforce dynamics, or industry trends, you're on the same path as **Blockbuster**. The world moves forward—with or without you.

Artificial intelligence (AI) is reshaping industries. It's automating tasks, streamlining workflows, and changing how decisions are made. At a recent conference, a presenter told the audience, *"The shift isn't coming—it's already here."* As a leader, the real question is: *How are you evolving alongside it?*

Staying relevant requires intentional investment in yourself. The most successful leaders don't rely on past achievements. They **learn,**

adapt, and position themselves ahead of change. Whether it's mastering new technologies, expanding your expertise, or adjusting to new leadership dynamics, growth is a choice.

It's a lesson I had to learn myself. I was given opportunities to develop new skills, but because I lacked interest, I never fully invested. Later, when I needed those skills, I found myself playing catch-up instead of being prepared.

Blockbuster could have redefined its model. Kodak could have led the digital revolution. But they relied too heavily on what had worked before instead of preparing for what was coming next.

You face the same choice. You can hold on to old ways of thinking, assuming past success will carry you forward, or you can commit to continuous growth, staying ahead of trends, and evolving as the world changes. Trust me, as a leader, it will benefit you.

The Cost of Stagnation

Resisting change breeds complacency. And in today's world, stagnation isn't just a setback—it's a liability. A stagnant organization struggles to attract top talent, adapt to consumer needs, and compete in a changing market.

The same applies to personal leadership. If you're leading the same way you were five years ago, it's time for a reality check. The workforce has changed, expectations have shifted, and technology continues to reshape business. **Those who refuse to evolve will be replaced by those who do.**

How to Stay Ahead of the Curve

Being future-focused isn't just about predicting what's next—it's about equipping yourself and your organization to succeed in a constantly evolving landscape. Here's how you can stay ahead:

1. Commit to Lifelong Learning

Industries are shifting faster than ever, and the best leaders are those who never stop learning. Make it a habit to read industry reports, attend conferences, take online courses, and engage with thought leaders. Don't wait for someone to tell you what's relevant—seek it out.

2. Encourage Innovation Within Your Team

A future-focused leader creates a culture of adaptability. That means empowering your team to bring forward new ideas, experiment with different ways of working, and challenge outdated processes. Organizations that foster innovation stay ahead, while those that resist it become outdated.

3. Build a Network That Expands Your Perspective

Surround yourself with people who challenge your thinking. Engage with professionals from different industries, attend networking events, and be open to perspectives outside your usual circle. Some of the best innovations come from cross-industry insights.

4. Leverage Technology as an Advantage

Artificial intelligence, automation, and digital transformation are not just buzzwords—they're redefining how businesses operate. If you're not exploring how technology can enhance your leadership, streamline your operations, or improve decision-making, you're missing out on growth opportunities.

5. Prepare for the Unexpected

The COVID-19 pandemic taught us all that the unexpected can and will happen. Organizations that were agile and prepared for remote work, supply chain disruptions, and market shifts survived. Those that weren't struggled to stay afloat. Future-focused leadership means having contingency plans and being able to pivot when necessary.

By expanding your skills, strengthening your presence, and investing in your well-being, you create a legacy that lasts far beyond any job title. So, I'll leave this with you:

> What will your legacy be, and what are you doing today to make it a reality?

Step outside your comfort zone. Own your growth. Elevate yourself—and in doing so, elevate everyone around you. Because at the end of the day, you are worth it. And damn it, *own your worth!*

PART FOUR: RELATIONSHIP BUILDING

The reputation of how you make someone feel lasts longer than what you make them do.

CHAPTER ELEVEN
Changing Leadership Colors

> "Growth doesn't occur by staying comfortable in the shadows; it blossoms when exposed to the rain and nurtured by the light."

Leadership is an incredible journey—one filled with guiding change, celebrating progress, learning from setbacks, and making a meaningful impact on others. During the early years of my career, I learned that titles and authority are just one aspect of leadership. The real impact comes from influence, leading by example, and finding an approach that aligns with who you are. But if there's one lesson that stands out the most, it's this: managing people is, without a doubt, the hardest part of leadership. No matter how authentic or well-intentioned you are, navigating the people side of leadership will test every fiber of your being.

When stepping into leadership, I gravitated toward Servant Leadership—rolling up my sleeves, working alongside my team, and doing whatever it took to get the job done. It felt right, but over time, I realized this approach had a major flaw: I was carrying too much of the load while failing to hold others accountable. And that, I quickly learned, is a leadership mistake that can have serious consequences.

The Power of Accountability

Rule enforcement in accountability often is misconstrued by leaders who think leading is making people do something. It's not. Accountability is a simple but cumbersome task: ensure that everyone understands and demonstrates their commitment to the team's success. When embedded in a team's culture, people take ownership of their work, follow through on commitments, and feel a sense of responsibility for shared goals. It becomes collaborative rather than individual.

On the flip side, when accountability is missing, chaos takes over. Expectations become unclear, deadlines are missed, and resentment builds when people feel like others aren't pulling their weight. And trust me—people notice.

One of my biggest leadership lessons in accountability came from a situation with a team member—let's call her Abigail. Abigail was personable and fantastic with students, but she had a habit of strolling in late and, on occasion, "forgetting" to clock in. At first, I brushed it off, thinking, "We're all professionals; I expect you to act accordingly." Plus, who actually enjoys a micromanager?

But here's where reality smacked me in the face—while I was trying to avoid being overbearing, my team was taking notes. And not the good kind. It's like when you're in a group project, and one person contributes nothing, yet still gets the same grade. Sure, the work gets done, but the frustration? That festers. The inconsistency created resentment, and my reluctance to enforce accountability was at the root of it.

This experience forced me to rethink my leadership approach. I had to strike a balance between trust and accountability—ensuring fairness while keeping the team dynamic intact. Once I set clearer expectations and introduced performance tracking, things improved. Unfortunately, Abigail ultimately chose to leave, unable to meet the new standards. But the lesson was clear: clarity, fairness, and consistency weren't just buzzwords—they were essential for success.

The Spectrum of Leadership Styles

In the beginning, I believed there was a universal leadership style—a one-size-fits-all approach that would work for every team member in every situation. But experience quickly taught me otherwise. People are unique, and so are the challenges leaders face. Relying on a single leadership style can limit your ability to connect, inspire, and drive results. The most effective leaders adapt and diversify their approach, using the right style at the right time to bring out the best in their teams.

Just as people have different personalities, they also respond to different leadership styles. Some thrive under authoritative leadership, where a leader provides clear direction and a strong vision. These individuals excel when they understand expectations and see how their work contributes to the bigger picture.[20] Others prefer a more democratic approach, where collaboration and shared decision-making take center stage.[21] For them, being heard and playing an active role in shaping outcomes is key. Some work best under coaching leadership, where the focus is on growth and development. A coaching leader mentors, guides, and helps individuals reach their potential—particularly valuable for those eager to advance in their careers.[22] Meanwhile, affiliative leadership centers on harmony, trust, and relationships.[23] This approach is especially effective during times of conflict or change, as it prioritizes empathy and connection over rigid structure.

One of the most important lessons I've learned is that sticking to a single leadership style can create disconnect and frustration. If I insisted on an authoritative approach with everyone, I'd risk alienating those who thrive in a more collaborative or coaching-driven environment. True leadership isn't about what makes you comfortable—it's about what makes your team successful.

I recall leading a team with varying levels of experience. Some members were seasoned professionals who thrived with autonomy, while others were just starting out and needed more hands-on guidance. A one-size-fits-all approach would have left someone struggling. Instead, I adapted—providing mentorship where it was needed while stepping back to let experienced team members lead their own way. The result? A team that felt supported, empowered, and motivated to perform at their best. This experience led me to develop what I now call the Chameleon Concept of Leadership.

The Chameleon Concept of Leadership

A chameleon is one of the most fascinating creatures in the animal kingdom. It's best known for its ability to change colors, but there's much more to this creature than meets the eye. The way a chameleon navigates its environment holds valuable lessons for leaders who seek to be effective, adaptable, and attuned to their team's needs. There are three specific characteristics that I want to highlight regarding this concept: adaptability, awareness, and balance.

1. Adaptability: Adjusting to the Environment

Contrary to popular belief, chameleons don't change color to blend in—they do so to regulate body temperature, communicate emotions, and respond to their surroundings. Similarly, great leaders don't adapt just to "fit in" but to respond to challenges, communicate effectively, and create balance within their teams.

A leader who refuses to adapt—clinging to a single leadership style—risks losing touch with their team. Workplaces aren't static; dynamics shift, challenges evolve, and what worked yesterday might not work tomorrow. Great leaders pay attention to team morale, engagement, and individual needs, adjusting their approach accordingly. Adaptability ensures that leaders remain relevant, effective, and able to guide their teams through change.

2. Awareness: Observing Before Acting

A chameleon's eyes move independently, scanning its environment for opportunities and threats. It can assess its surroundings without making rash movements, ensuring it reacts wisely. Let's consider one of my favorite comic book characters, Spider-Man. Spider-Man's Spidey Sense is one of his most powerful abilities—it's that invisible alarm, an instinctive tingle at the back of his mind that warns him when danger is near. Before he even sees the threat, he feels it. His senses heighten, time seems to slow, and every nerve in his body fires off an alert: *Something's wrong. Pay attention.* It's this awareness that often saves him, allowing him to react before disaster strikes.

In leadership, having that same heightened sense—minus the radioactive spider bite—can make all the difference. A great leader develops an instinct for reading the room, sensing when morale is low, spotting frustration before it boils over, and recognizing when a team member is struggling in silence. Just like Spider-Man doesn't wait for the villain to strike before taking action, strong leaders don't wait for problems to explode before addressing them. They stay alert, anticipate, and act—because in both superhero work and leadership, awareness is the key to success.

But beyond awareness, great leaders also listen. They gather insights, ask the right questions, and make informed decisions to ensure their approach aligns with the needs of those they lead.

3. Balance: Regulating Leadership Energy

A chameleon's color changes help regulate body temperature—turning lighter in hot conditions to cool down and darker when it needs warmth. This is a powerful analogy for leadership. Good leaders adjust their energy, engagement, and level of involvement based on the needs of their team.

Some employees thrive with autonomy, needing little guidance, while others require hands-on coaching. Some situations call for a firm, directive approach, while others demand empathy and patience. Just like the chameleon, a leader knows when to be hands-on and when to step back. Overexerting in the wrong areas can lead to burnout, while under-engaging can lead to team disengagement.

The C.H.A.N.G.E. Framework: A Guide to Adaptive Leadership

To fully embrace the Chameleon Concept of Leadership, I developed the C.H.A.N.G.E. Framework—a structured approach to navigating adaptability in leadership. By definition, *change* means "to make a shift from one to another," but in leadership, it goes deeper. Change is the conscious act of growth, the willingness to evolve, and the courage to shift perspectives when needed. Without timely access to the right leadership strategies, growth can be stunted, causing setbacks in your leadership journey. The C.H.A.N.G.E. Framework helps prevent that by providing six essential pillars that empower leaders to adapt with purpose and lead with authenticity.

1. **Capability Recognition** (Inner Strength & Potential; Self-Awareness & Growth; Service-Driven Leadership) – Everything you need to succeed as a leader is already within you. Start with self-awareness, confidence, and a commitment to personal growth, as the best leaders don't wait for validation—they recognize their potential and work on refining their strengths.

2. **Heightened Awareness** (Empathy-Driven Leadership; Active Listening & Observation; Avoiding Leadership Blind Spots) – Take time to understand the people you lead. Learn their aspirations, values, and what they need from you as their leader. Neglecting your team's needs leads to disengagement and dissatisfaction.

3. **Adaptive Timing** (Adaptive Leadership; Situational Awareness; Culture & Productivity) – Once you understand your team,

adapt your leadership approach. Some employees need frequent check-ins, while others thrive with independence. Knowing when to step in, step back, or step up makes all the difference in leadership effectiveness.

4. **Naming Vulnerability** (Emotional Connections; Strategic Accountability; Trust through Tact) – Being adaptable and responsive to your team's needs can be exhausting. Leaders must recognize when they are drained, maintain emotional intelligence, and handle challenges with tact and self-awareness. To do this, you must be honest with who you are as an individual and where you are as a leader. Being vulnerable to share when you don't have all the answers builds strength and credibility with your team.

5. **Growth through Renewal** (Authenticity in Leading; Mental & Emotional Renewal; The Power of Unplugging) – Just as a chameleon returns to its natural color after adapting, leaders must also return to their authentic selves. Unplugging, recharging, and embracing personal identity outside of work prevents burnout and keeps you effective.

6. **Evolution through Reflection** (Self-reflection & Improvement; Continuous Learning) – Leadership is a continuous process. Always ask: *Am I leading effectively? Am I making an impact?* Growth requires consistency. By repeating and refining these steps, you evolve into a stronger, more adaptable leader each day.

The ability to adapt is crucial in leadership, helping to avoid common pitfalls and ensure long-term success.

> Leadership isn't about rigid rules or a single "right" way to lead—it's about understanding people, situations, and the nuances that make each team unique. A simple but practical approach can make all the difference.

As we conclude this chapter, I want to share a leadership experience with you. A few years ago, I mentored a manager named Brian, who had always prided himself on being a strong leader—organized, efficient, and confident in his decisions. His team met their goals, but something wasn't clicking. Meetings felt one-sided, innovation was lacking, and employee engagement was steadily declining. Turnover was increasing, and he couldn't figure out why. During one of our coaching sessions, I asked him a simple but revealing question: *Do you know what your team needs from you?* He immediately responded with a list of expectations, metrics, and performance goals, but he couldn't answer anything about his team members as individuals. That was the problem—he was leading based on what was comfortable for him, not what worked for his people.

One afternoon, during a routine check-in, a team member hesitated before speaking, then finally admitted, "Brian, we don't always feel like we can bring ideas to you. It seems like things have to be done your way." The words stung, but they opened his eyes. That night, he sat down with a notebook, writing each team member's name and asking himself: *What are their strengths? What motivates them? How do they prefer to be led?* The exercise revealed gaps he had ignored for too long. The next morning, instead of coming in with directives, he came in with questions, ready to listen, learn, and lead with awareness. Over time, Brian realized that some team members thrived with more autonomy, while others needed more guidance.

He adjusted, he adapted, and he transformed—not just himself, but his leadership impact.

Now, it's your turn. You've been introduced to leadership styles, the *Chameleon Concept of Leadership*, and given insights into the elements embedded within it. However, now I want you to take a moment to consider your own style and the people you lead. On a piece of paper, write down your team members—the ones you have direct responsibility for leading—and capture these questions: *What are three character traits they possess? How are they as individuals? What are their interests as people? How do they prefer to be led? And most importantly, what do they need from a supervisor?* If you can't answer these questions, they are ones you should get answers to. They will help you along the way to meet their needs and develop a lasting professional relationship. Leadership is not about proving your authority; it is about elevating those around you. Are you leading for comfort, or are you leading for impact? Your next step begins now.

CHAPTER TWELVE
The Power of Words

> "A voice has many options: it can choose to remain silent or choose to be heard. In either case, the consequence for your future is inevitable."

I was about fifteen years old when I first heard Mother Brown say it. She was one of the elders in our church—the kind of woman whose presence commanded both respect and warmth. Her silver-streaked hair was always neatly pinned, and her Sunday hats were the stuff of legends. On this particular Sunday afternoon, she was sitting outside the fellowship hall between our morning and afternoon service, fanning herself with a church program, when she saw me storming across the church, arms crossed, my face scrunched up in frustration.

I had just told my friend exactly what I thought about his terrible singing—word for word, no sugarcoating—and let's just say, he didn't take it well.

Mother Brown chuckled, the kind of deep, knowing laugh that made you pause. She waved me over, patting the empty space beside her on the bench. *"Come sit down, baby."*

I plopped down, still fuming.

She tilted her head, eyes kind but sharp. "*Now, what got you looking like you lost a fight with your own shadow?*"

I sighed. "*I was just telling the truth! But now he's mad at me.*"

She nodded, rocking slightly as she fanned herself. "*Mmm-hmm. Truth is good, but let me tell you something—truth without grace is just noise.*" She tapped her fan against her knee. "*It's not what you say, child. It's how you say it.*"

I frowned, letting her words sit for a moment.

She smiled, leaning in just a little. "*If you want people to listen, you got to speak in a way they want to hear. Otherwise, you're just talking at them, not to them.*"

Then she sat back, as if the matter was settled, and went right back to fanning herself, humming an old hymn under her breath.

I didn't fully understand it then, but years later—standing in a meeting, carefully choosing my words in a tough conversation—I heard her voice clear as day.

And she was right. Every time.

Back then, and more ever now, I've come to understand just how profoundly our communication shapes the people and environments around us—especially in leadership.

The way we communicate can either uplift or undermine those we lead, leaving lasting impressions. Studies show that 69% of employees say they would work harder if they felt their efforts were better recognized.[25] A simple acknowledgment of someone's strengths or a word of appreciation can ignite motivation, making individuals feel valued and inspired to go the extra mile. Conversely, careless criticism or dismissive remarks can extinguish that same enthusiasm in seconds. I've seen talented individuals shut down after an idea was met with immediate skepticism or undue criticism. Within academia, where innovation thrives on open dialogue, leaders should be mindful of how their words set the tone for trust, collaboration, and engagement.

Your Words Travel Further Than You Think

The power of words has always been undeniable, but in today's digital era, their impact is magnified. Growing up, I'd hear the phrase, *"Your tongue is like the rudder of a boat. How you control it determines how far you will go."* Those sayings never truly resonated with me until later in life. It's like something magically clicked and all of the wisdom shared then became relevant now.

Insight like the aforementioned shaped how I conversed with people. Especially, when I realized that the privacy of our conversations are no longer confined to offices, boardrooms, or faculty meetings. Our statements can be shared, scrutinized, and reinterpreted by a global audience within seconds. And, people are watching and listening to hear what we say. A single comment—whether in an email, a speech, or even a tweet—can be dissected beyond its original context, sometimes manipulated to fit a different narrative altogether.

This reality extends across industries. In politics, for example, unfiltered communication has become a powerful but dangerous tool. Like during a debate, a leader might call their opponent a liar or blame them for all the problems in the country. While this kind of talk can grab attention, it can also cause big problems. Using emotionally charged language to sway public opinion, sometimes at the expense of truth and unity, can lead to misunderstandings, fights, or even violence. When leaders use words like this, people might start to doubt if they are honest or trustworthy. A recent Pew Research Center study found that 63% of Americans believe political discourse has become more divisive due to inflammatory rhetoric.[26] The same risks exist across all business industries. Whether in a public statement or a private conversation, the words of leaders carry immense weight. A poorly phrased email or an offhand remark can erode trust and alienate key stakeholders, while thoughtful and intentional communication can foster loyalty, morale, and institutional cohesion.

A Lesson in Leadership: Choosing Words with Care

The difference between a leader who builds bridges and one who burns them often comes down to communication. I've observed leaders face backlash not just for *what* they said, but *how* they said it. The lesson that Mother Brown taught me back in the day. One recent example involved a university president whose statement about faculty concerns was perceived as dismissive. The resulting controversy wasn't solely about the content—it was about tone. Faculty and staff felt unheard, and the disconnect sparked a wave of mistrust that extended far beyond the initial statement which stifled his ability to move the institution forward.

Conversely, I've witnessed leaders diffuse difficult situations with empathy and transparency. Recently, a colleague, overwhelmed by workload and tight deadlines, sent an email addressing an error made by another team member. The tone was derogatory and blameful, reflecting their frustration. Reading it, I sensed a lack of collaboration and a missed opportunity to address the issue constructively— perhaps through offering training or initiating a discussion. While I felt offended by the email, I knew that responding in the same tone would only escalate the situation.

Instead, I acknowledged their frustration in my response but emphasized that our shared goal was to create a workplace where we could all succeed and minimize errors. By redirecting the conversation and adopting a collaborative approach, the sender responded apologetically, admitting that her approach was influenced by the pressure she was under. This experience reinforced the importance of choosing our words thoughtfully, even in frustrating moments.

> The lesson here is simple yet profound: words are never just words. They carry weight, shape perceptions, and influence outcomes. For some, they can trigger past traumas or reinforce negative assumptions. For others, they can inspire confidence, drive innovation, and create environments where people feel valued.

Building Trust Through Words

Great leaders understand that every interaction—whether spoken, written, or posted online—offers an opportunity to either build trust or break it. And in the ever-evolving business landscape, trust is a leader's most valuable asset.

Effective communication is vital to efficacy in leadership because it helps to generate rapport, build trust, and encourage collaboration towards a common goal.[27]

A study examining the relationship between leadership styles in higher education institutions and academic staff's job satisfaction found that transformational leadership styles, characterized by effective communication, have a positive and strong effect on job satisfaction.[28] The way leaders communicate profoundly impacts their teams and organizations. By being mindful of our words and their delivery, we can foster environments of trust, collaboration, and growth.

In Education where the mission is to educate and inspire, communication must reflect the values they uphold—integrity, empathy, and respect for diverse perspectives. Every interaction must be intentional, as words have the potential to either strengthen the community or irreparably harm it. Eyes will always be on you, but they can close. On the other hand, ears are always open, and they are waiting to be filled by your words. Therefore, what we say must be chosen wisely.

CHAPTER THIRTEEN
Your Choice: Respond or React

> "Everyone has a button that can be pushed. However, what happens when it's pushed depends on how the device is programmed."

People have often remarked on how calm I remain in high-pressure situations. To me, it's a gift—one that has allowed me to navigate challenges and escape potentially volatile situations. In many ways, I see it as a defense mechanism, a way to protect myself and others from unnecessary conflict. Yet, I've realized it's a personal strategy that helps me lead better.

Controlling your emotions, like when you want to yell at a team member for missing a deadline or making a careless mistake, is a true test of leadership. Instead of reacting in frustration, taking a moment to breathe and address the issue with clarity can turn a tense moment into a learning opportunity. A measured response not only keeps the team's morale intact but also reinforces a culture of accountability and respect.

As a leader, you set the tone for your team, and how you react to stress, conflict, or adversity directly influences the atmosphere and morale. When you remain composed, others feel secure and are more likely to stay focused and productive. On the other hand, losing control—whether through anger, frustration, or impatience—can lead to chaos, undermine trust, and even create fear.

During a recent online exploration, I stumbled across a profound analogy by Dr. Martin Luther King, Jr. As an advocate for peace, he often shared wisdom that remains deeply relevant, including his comparison between a thermometer and a thermostat.

Like many, I sometimes start my day by scrolling through social media to catch up on the world. On this particular morning, I came across a speaker discussing this powerful concept from Dr. King—one that immediately captured my attention. He explained that a thermometer merely reflects the temperature of its surroundings, passively reacting to external conditions. When the environment heats up, so does the thermometer; when it cools down, it follows suit. A thermostat, however, operates differently. It doesn't just measure the temperature—it regulates it, actively shaping the environment rather than being shaped by it.

As I listened, I found myself reflecting on how often leaders fall into the trap of being thermometers—absorbing the emotions, stress, and chaos around them. When tensions rise, they rise too. When uncertainty looms, they waver. They react to circumstances instead of influencing them. I realized that, in moments of pressure, I had been guilty of the same—allowing external noise to dictate my internal state.

But the most effective leaders—the ones who inspire, empower, and drive change—operate as thermostats. They don't just react; they respond. They remain steady in turmoil, adjusting the emotional and mental climate around them rather than being controlled by it. They bring clarity to confusion, calm to crisis, and purpose to chaos.

Dr. King's analogy serves as a powerful reminder about setting the standard for stability. A thermostat doesn't ignore the temperature—it senses, acknowledges, and regulates it. Likewise, great leaders don't suppress challenges or emotions; they understand them, process them, and respond with intention rather than impulse.

As I set my phone down, a question lingered in my mind: Am I leading like a thermometer, merely reacting to everything around me? Or am I leading like a thermostat, intentionally setting the tone and shaping the environment? That moment was a reality check—I had been unregulated, allowing external factors to dictate my response. It was a grounding realization, a subtle yet powerful reminder that responding with wisdom and purpose always creates a greater impact than simply reacting in the moment.

A Demonstration of Self-Control in Leadership

Years ago, I learned a profound lesson while working in customer service, an industry where the phrase "the customer is always right" was practically gospel. To be honest, that slogan didn't always sit well with me because, let's face it, sometimes the customer wasn't right. But what stuck with me more than the mantra was the importance of understanding the difference between "responding" and "reacting." That distinction would prove critical one evening during my shift.

It was a typical busy evening, and I was helping the front-line staff manage the dinner rush. I remember it clearly—a customer, a white man, placed a special order for a deluxe cheeseburger with no onions. The order was entered correctly, and when it was ready, it was assembled on his tray along with the rest of his items. He took his tray, found a seat in the dining area, and began to eat. A few minutes later, he came back, holding the burger in one hand and wearing a look of pure frustration.

With a raised voice, he yelled directly at me, "I asked for no onions, and this sandwich has onions on it!" I instantly acknowledged the mistake and apologized for the error. The request had been overlooked somewhere between taking his order and the kitchen preparing it. I apologized again, telling him I would correct his order. But before I could fix the issue, he threw the burger at me, the lettuce and tomato splattering across my uniform. As he stormed out of the restaurant, he called me the one word no Black person ever wants to hear: "nigger."

Time seemed to freeze. My heart pounded, my hands clenched, and every fiber of my being screamed to react. The insult cut deep—real deep—not just because I'd never heard it before, but because he had the audacity to say it. That word. Unacceptable in any context. But what stunned me even more was that his anger had no justification— I was only trying to make things right.

I stood there, replaying the moment in my head. *Did he really just say that to me? Did he just toss his sandwich at me like that was okay?* The thoughts wouldn't stop racing. But then, reality hit me—the eyes of my team were locked on me, waiting, watching, measuring my response.

In that instant, I faced a choice: *Do I react, letting my anger take the wheel? Or do I take control, respond with intention, and stay true to who I am?*

Reacting might have meant shouting back, escalating the situation, or even risking my job. Responding meant taking a breath, staying calm, and showing others—including my team—how to handle pressure and adversity with integrity. I chose to respond. I cleaned up the mess, moved forward with the evening, and let the customer's actions to speak for themselves. Pure ignorance and disgrace. He never returned to that restaurant, and I never lost the pride I felt in staying composed.

Assessing Key Characteristics of Control

I shared that story with you because it was a vulnerable moment that tested my leadership. I'm sure you know—now more than ever—that there's a clear difference between reacting and responding. Understanding that difference can have a significant impact on how a team operates.

This ability to respond, rather than react, is a huge part of emotional intelligence. Leaders who can maintain their composure, no matter the situation, are better equipped to guide their teams through both calm and turbulent times. For instance, think about a manager whose temperament fluctuates daily—one day they're calm and supportive, and the next, they might be irritable or short-tempered. It's exhausting for the team, and the constant unpredictability can create a tense work environment. Team members might feel on edge, unsure of how their actions will be perceived. This unpredictability impacts not just the team's morale but the overall culture. A culture where reactions dominate over responses tends to breed anxiety and inconsistency, leaving employees uncertain of how they will be treated on any given day. In contrast, a leader who consistently responds with thoughtfulness and stability creates a culture of trust and calm.

To maintain emotional control in the face of challenges, leaders can adopt several key strategies. One powerful approach is *mindfulness*, which helps center the mind and reduce impulsive reactions. Studies have shown that practicing mindfulness significantly enhances emotional regulation.[29]

Another effective technique is the "*pause-and-reflect*" method. When confronted with a stressful situation, take a brief moment before responding – it can make all the difference. This intentional pause allows you to collect your thoughts, assess the situation, and choose a measured response rather than reacting in the heat of the moment. By staying emotionally grounded, leaders not only enhance their own effectiveness but also cultivate a stable, positive environment where their teams can thrive.

I want to remind you of this: how we respond to the actions of others can shape the environment we lead.

> People are always watching.
> People are always waiting.
> People are always wondering,
> how you will navigate difficult spaces.

Understanding that we are human, we can't ignore the hurt or pretend it doesn't affect us. However, we have the power to rise above the chaos, demonstrate resilience, and lead with grace—even when it feels impossible.

CHAPTER FOURTEEN
Intentional Leadership

> "How you show up matters. How you stay matters more. And, how you remain afterwards matters the most."

Have you ever found yourself in a meeting, surrounded by people who are eagerly waiting for you to speak, and then... you freeze? Not because you don't have anything to say, but because the moment feels too important. You want to get it right. You want to connect. But you don't want to overshare. So, you start saying something... then pause, say more, and before you know it, you're telling them things they didn't need to know. Now, everyone's a little uncomfortable, and you're wondering if you should've just kept your mouth shut.

Let me tell you, I've been there. As a leader, the weight of your words are significant. The information you share can either strengthen your team or cause unnecessary confusion. Being influential requires intentionality—acting with purpose and clarity in everything you do, especially how you communicate with your team. It's one of the most vital aspects of effective leadership, yet one that's often overlooked.

As a leader, I'd often get caught up in the desire to be "relatable" or "open." I'd share details thinking it would build trust, only to realize

I was inadvertently creating anxiety. I'd share a staffing issue or a project delay in a way that made the team feel like they had to fix it—adding unnecessary pressure. I wasn't thinking about how my words affected them. This kind of communication does the opposite of what you want. Instead of empowering them, you overwhelm them. It was at this moment I began to realize that people don't have to know the full story, only the intricate pieces that mattered. Think of it as curating a playlist for your team's morale. Too many songs (or too much information) can make the experience chaotic. But just the right mix can create the perfect atmosphere—focused, empowered, and moving in sync toward success. This is why you must be intentional about what you say and how you say it as a leader.

The Right Mix of Information

You may think sharing every detail with your team makes you more transparent. However, oversharing can create confusion, stress, and unnecessary complications. I recall a discussion with a colleague about what information should be included in a report to the board. They wanted to provide everything possible based on the request. Over time, I discovered that sometimes being brief is enough to meet the task's requirements. As a policy trainer, I learned to present information at a high level while anticipating deeper questions that may arise later. Providing too much detail can overwhelm the audience, forcing them to spend unnecessary time deciphering the content. My colleague chose to include an excessive amount of information in the report. As a result, the back-and-forth for additional clarification dragged on for over a week.

So, how do you avoid falling into that trap like my colleague?

First, ask yourself: Does this person need to know this? When handling a staffing issue, sharing every detail—like who said what in a meeting or how the department is reorganizing—can create unnecessary panic. Instead, focus on what matters: *"There's a staffing challenge, and we're working to resolve it. I'll keep you updated."* Simple, clear, and solution-focused.

Oversharing can lead to distractions and unnecessary concerns when your team needs to stay focused on their work. As a leader, your role is to guide, not overwhelm. Keep essential information front and center, allowing your team to stay engaged while leadership handles the details. This approach fosters clarity, confidence, and productivity.

Intentional Word Choice: Less is More

Think about the last time you were frustrated with someone—whether it was a missed deadline or a project that wasn't going according to plan. Did your words reflect the situation clearly, or did they add fuel to the fire? If we're honest, we've all had moments where we blurt out words we immediately regret. That's why it's so important to be intentional with your word choice – pause and reflect. The language you use not only reflects your leadership style but also affects how your team feels and reacts.

Here's an example: Imagine addressing someone who missed a deadline. Saying, *"You missed the deadline,"* immediately places blame. But if you say, *"I noticed the deadline wasn't met. Let's talk about what happened,"* it shifts the tone. See the difference? This small change in language shows empathy and keeps the conversation solution-focused. I've used this approach to ensure my team didn't feel attacked, but instead felt supported in finding a resolution.

Consider another example: If a project is running behind schedule, don't just say, *"This project is behind."* Instead, try saying, *"We're behind, but I think we can catch up by reallocating some tasks. What do you think?"* This encourages collaboration, fosters clarity, and helps the team feel engaged and invested in the process.

Our words have power—whether we're aware of it or not. That's why every conversation is an opportunity to lead with intention. You can't afford to speak on autopilot, and honestly, it's one of the reasons I've always hated hearing people justify others' actions by saying, "He or she just speaks their mind!" These days, we need everyone to keep every part of their mind. So yes, being mindful is key to being intentional with our words—and trust me, it makes all the difference.

The Art of Listening: Be Present

Speaking is just one part of communication. If you really want to lead with intention, you have to listen. And I mean really listen—like, fully engage, put down the phone, and tune in to what the person is saying.

In a world where we're often multitasking and rushing to the next thing, listening with intent is rare. But it's impactful when you do it right. Think about it—how often do you find yourself zoning out during a conversation, only to pretend you heard the important stuff? Or maybe you're just waiting for the other person to finish talking so you can get your point across. Guilty as charged, right?

Listening is more than just hearing words. We must intentionally seek to understand the message behind them. When someone comes to you with a concern, give them your full attention. Don't think about how you're going to respond. Instead, focus on what they're saying and reflect back what you've heard. A simple response like, "So you're concerned about the project timeline. Is that right?" can make all the difference. It shows respect, encourages dialogue, and builds trust—critical elements of strong leadership.

You know what else helps? When you listen, you gain better insights into your team's needs. This allows you to address problems proactively before they become bigger issues.

As an exercise, put this in practice during your next conversation with a friend, colleague, or team member. Listen to what they say and reflect back to let them know you were paying attention. The more you practice, the easier it'll become to implement.

Clarity and Accountability: Lead with Solutions

When you're communicating clarity is key. But so is accountability. Leaders don't have time for long-winded explanations or vague complaints. They need solutions, not more problems.

There's something powerful about the phrase, "Let me take care of that for you." It's simple, direct, and carries the weight of accountability. In a LinkedIn interview, former President Barack Obama spoke about the kind of leaders he values—not just those who can articulate problems, but those who step up and solve them. Anyone can point out what's wrong. The real value lies in those who say, *"I've got it. Let me handle that."*

That statement is the difference between leadership that simply observes and leadership that moves things forward. Think about any workplace you've been in. There are always two types of people: those who narrate problems like a play-by-play announcer and those who quietly roll up their sleeves and figure it out. The latter are the ones who keep the wheels turning, the ones who make leadership smoother because they don't just identify roadblocks—they clear them.

The best leaders are problem-solvers. They don't just identify the issue; they come with ideas and a plan. And guess what? When you present solutions, others are more likely to take action.

The Power of Positivity: Make Feedback Work for You

If you've ever been on the receiving end of a harsh critique, you know it doesn't feel great. But here's the thing: tough conversations don't have to be negative. Feedback, when delivered with positivity, can be an opportunity for growth.

Think of feedback as a sandwich. You start with something positive, then offer constructive criticism, and wrap it up with another positive. This isn't just fluff—it's an intentional way to keep your team motivated and moving forward. Starting with praise shows that you see the effort they're putting in, and ending on a positive note reinforces your commitment to their success.

For example, if a project didn't meet expectations, try saying something like, "I really appreciate the hard work you put into this project. Let's discuss a few ways we can improve the outcome together." This approach lets them know you're invested in their growth and not just pointing out what went wrong.

Our people need us to show up—not to solve their problems, but to help them find solutions. That requires being intentional—deliberate in our actions, words, and relationships.

Whether sharing information, addressing a challenge, or giving feedback, approach it with intention. Your words and actions shape your team's culture and define your leadership.

> It's not just what you say—it's how, when, and why you say it. Every conversation is an opportunity to lead with purpose.

The Path of Unshaken Leadership

As your written mentor, I've shared my vulnerable experiences—not to put my flaws on display, but to remind you that we're all imperfect and still capable of growth. Perfection isn't the goal here—resilience is. A resilient leader bounces back, adapts, and moves forward, no matter the challenge.

You messed up? So what. Made the wrong call? So what. Upset someone along the way? Okay... that's inevitable. Mistakes aren't failures; they're opportunities—to refine your skills, build resilience, and unlock your full potential.

The most effective leaders aren't measured by how many times they stumble, but by how they rise—each time, stronger, wiser, and more determined. So, with every misstep, evolve. With every challenge, learn. And with every opportunity, be grateful. Leadership is a gift, and this book is here to remind you that no matter where you are in your journey, you have the power to rise, learn, and lead with confidence.

Before we part ways, let me leave you with this final story: A young man, discouraged by his countless failures in business, once said, "I've failed more times than I care to count, but each time I learn something new. I've learned to keep going." That man was Thomas Edison, whose failures didn't define him—they propelled him toward success.

Like Edison, you will stumble. You will fail. But if you keep learning, adapting, and pushing forward, the best version of yourself as a leader is waiting on the other side. Keep going—you've got this.

PART FIVE:
THE UNSHAKEN
LEADER

I am
now confident
in the mistakes,
lessons, and
opportunities.
They all
created wisdom.

Conclusion

> "I never knew my potential until I embraced who I was. It was in that discovery that my confidence strengthened, and my impact radiated."

As we draw this journey through the pages of *Unshaken Leadership: A Practical Blueprint for Overcoming Challenges, Learning from Mistakes, and Growing in Confidence* to a close, it is essential to reflect on the core themes that have emerged. The words "unshaken" and "leadership" resonate profoundly within the context of our exploration. To be unshaken implies a steadfastness in the face of adversity, a resilience that allows one to maintain clarity and purpose even when external circumstances threaten to destabilize. Leadership, on the other hand, is not merely about occupying a position of authority; it is about influencing, inspiring, and nurturing those around you. It requires a deep understanding of oneself and the courage to act in accordance with that understanding.

Throughout this book, we have delved into the significance of being confident in who you are as a person. Confidence is not merely an innate trait, but a conscious decision made daily. It is about embracing your uniqueness and recognizing your worth. This idea challenges the pervasive notion that one must conform to external expectations to be a leader. Instead, true leadership flourishes when individuals embrace their authenticity and allow that to guide their actions.

Consider the story of Maya, a young woman who found herself in a high-pressure role at a community-based organization. Initially, she struggled with self-doubt, often questioning her abilities and decisions. Each mistake felt like a monumental failure, and she often looked to her peers and superiors for validation. However, as she began to cultivate a deeper understanding of herself, she realized that confidence stems from within. Maya started to view her mistakes as opportunities for growth rather than as reflections of her worth. By embracing her imperfections, she became more open to learning and sought feedback from her team, which fostered a culture of collaboration and trust.

As Maya's journey illustrates, growing in wisdom is a vital aspect of leadership. Wisdom is not simply accumulated knowledge; it is the application of that knowledge to become a better person and leader. It involves the ability to reflect on experiences, to learn from them, and to apply those lessons moving forward. This iterative process of learning and growing is what sets unshaken leaders apart. They do not shy away from challenges; instead, they embrace them as opportunities for personal and professional development.

Moreover, the path of an unshaken leader is often marked by a commitment to continuous self-improvement. This commitment requires a daily refinement of one's decisions and actions. It involves taking the time to assess how one responds to challenges and actively seeking ways to enhance that response. For you, this might mean setting aside moments each week for self-reflection. Moments to journal about your experiences, noting what went well and what could be improved. This practice allows you to recognize patterns in your behavior and to adjust your approach accordingly.

Engaging in such reflective practices can also foster a greater sense of empathy and understanding toward others. When leaders acknowledge their own struggles and growth, they become more attuned to the challenges faced by their team members. This empathy strengthens relationships and builds a more cohesive team environment, where everyone feels valued and understood.

As we conclude, let us remember that leadership is not a destination but a journey—a continuous evolution of self-discovery, learning, and growth. The lessons learned throughout this book are not meant to be mere points to check off but rather principles to integrate into our daily lives. Embracing our identity, learning from our mistakes, and growing in wisdom are all integral to becoming unshaken leaders who can inspire others.

In this ever-changing world, the ability to remain unshaken amidst challenges is a powerful skill. It requires a blend of confidence, resilience, and a willingness to learn. As you move forward, challenge yourself to reflect on your journey, to embrace your authenticity, and to cultivate the wisdom needed to guide yourself and others.

To encapsulate the essence of **unshaken leadership**, consider this uplifting quote from John Quincy Adams:

> "If your actions inspire others to dream more, learn more, do more, and become more, you are a leader."

As your written mentor, I believe you are ready to take on the world of leadership. May your journey inspire not only your growth but also the growth of those around you. Embrace your path with confidence, and remember that every challenge is an opportunity to learn and grow.

THINK IT.
SPEAK IT.
MANIFEST IT.

Now go lead, *unshaken*.

End Notes

1. American Psychological Association. *2023 Work in America Survey: Workplaces as Engines of Psychological Health and Well-Being.* 2023. https://www.apa.org/pubs/reports/work-in-america/2023-workplace-health-well-being.
2. Sorenson, S. "How Employees' Strengths Make Your Company Stronger." *Gallup Workplace*, 2025. https://www.gallup.com/workplace/231605/employees-strengths-company-stronger.aspx.
3. Harvard Business Review. "Stop Screening Job Candidates' Social Media." *Harvard Business Review*, 2021. https://hbr.org/2021/09/stop-screening-job-candidates-social-media.
4. CareerBuilder. "70% of Employers Are Snooping Candidates' Social Media Profiles." *CareerBuilder*, 2018. https://www.careerbuilder.com/advice/blog/social-media-survey-2017.
5. Vatere, B. "Generation Z: Identity and Expression in the Digital World." *Medium Magazine*, 2021. https://medium.com/@bvatere/generation-z-identity-and-expression-in-the-digital-world-50d2b28df829.
6. Media Culture. "From Analog to Streaming: The Evolution of Gen X Media Habits." *Media Culture*, 2023. https://www.mediaculture.com/insights/from-analog-to-streaming-evolution-of-gen-x-media-habits.
7. Hsu, A. "America, We Have a Problem: People Aren't Feeling Engaged with Their Work." *NPR*, 2023. https://www.npr.org/2023/01/25/1150816271/employee-engagement-gallup-survey-workers-hybrid-remote.
8. Torrance, L. "The Link Between Change Management and Employee Engagement." *Prosci*, 2025.

https://www.prosci.com/blog/change-management-employee-engagement.

9. LSA Global. "5 Components and 4 Criteria of an Effective Strategic Vision Statement." *LSA Global*, 2025. https://lsaglobal.com/blog/5-components-4-criteria-effective-strategic-vision/.

10. McKinsey & Company. *Hybrid Work: Making It Fit with Your Diversity, Equity, and Inclusion Strategy*. 2022. https://www.mckinsey.com/capabilities/people-and-organizational-performance/our-insights/hybrid-work-making-it-fit-with-your-diversity-equity-and-inclusion-strategy.

11. Gallup, Inc. *State of the Global Workplace: 2024 Report*. 2024. https://www.gallup.com/workplace/349484/state-of-the-global-workplace.aspx.

12. Korn Ferry. *The Black P&L Leader: Insights and Lessons from Senior Black P&L Leaders in Corporate America*. 2019. https://www.kornferry.com/content/dam/kornferry-v2/featured-topics/pdf/korn-ferry_theblack-pl-leader.pdf.

13. Workforce Institute. *Mental Health at Work: Managers and Money*. 2023. https://www.ukg.com/resources/white-paper/mental-health-work-managers-and-money.

14. Bureau of Labor Statistics, U.S. Department of Labor. "Median Tenure with Current Employer Was 3.9 Years in January 2024." *The Economics Daily*, 2024. https://www.bls.gov/opub/ted/2024/median-tenure-with-current-employer-was-3-9-years-in-january-2024.htm.

15. LinkedIn Learning. *Building the Agile Future: L&D Puts People and Skills at the Center of Organizational Success. Workplace Learning Report*, 2023. https://learning.linkedin.com/content/dam/me/learning/en-us/pdfs/workplace-learning-report/LinkedIn-Learning_Workplace-Learning-Report-2023-EN.pdf.

16. LinkedIn Learning. *Building the Agile Future: L&D Puts People and Skills at the Center of Organizational Success. Workplace Learning Report*, 2023. https://learning.linkedin.com/content/dam/me/learning/en-

us/pdfs/workplace-learning-report/LinkedIn-Learning_Workplace-Learning-Report-2023-EN.pdf.
17. World Economic Forum. "Future of Jobs 2023: These Are the Most In-Demand Skills Now—and Beyond." *World Economic Forum*, 2023. https://www.weforum.org/stories/2023/05/future-of-jobs-2023-skills.
18. World Economic Forum. *The Future of Jobs Report 2023*. 2023. https://www.weforum.org/publications/the-future-of-jobs-report-2023/.
19. National Career College. "Emotional Intelligence in Leadership: Why It's Crucial for Effective Leadership." *National Career College Blog*, 2024. https://nccusa.edu/blog/the-role-of-emotional-intelligence-in-leadership/.
20. Humaans. "Goleman's Leadership Styles." *Humaans HR Glossary*, accessed 2024. https://humaans.io/hr-glossary/goleman-s-leadership-styles.
21. Personio. "Six Goleman Leadership Styles." *Personio HR Lexicon*, accessed 2024. https://www.personio.com/hr-lexicon/six-goleman-leadership-styles.
22. Sutcliffe, K., T. J. Vogus, and E. Dane. "Coaching Leadership and Its Impact on Professional Development: A Review." *BMC Medical Education* 17, no. 1 (2017): 1–12. https://bmcmededuc.biomedcentral.com/articles/10.1186/s12909-017-0995-z.
23. eHotelier. "The Six Different Leadership Styles." *eHotelier Insights*, January 30, 2022. https://insights.ehotelier.com/insights/2022/01/30/the-six-different-leadership-styles/.
24. Merriam-Webster. "Definition of Change." *Merriam-Webster Dictionary*, accessed 2025. https://www.merriam-webster.com/dictionary/change.
25. Vantage Circle. "Top 21 Most Important Employee Recognition Statistics in 2025." *Vantage Circle*, 2024. https://www.vantagecircle.com/en/blog/employee-recognition-statistics.

26. Pew Research Center. *Americans' Dismal Views of the Nation's Politics.* 2023.
    https://www.pewresearch.org/politics/2023/09/19/americans-dismal-views-of-the-nations-politics/.
27. Industry Leaders Magazine. "Unlocking Leadership Potential Through Strong Communication Skills." *Industry Leaders Magazine*, 2024.
    https://www.industryleadersmagazine.com/unlocking-leadership-potential-through-strong-communication-skills/.
28. Grossman, D. *Leadership Communication: 6 Skills That the Best Leaders Apply.* The Grossman Group, 2024.
    https://www.yourthoughtpartner.com/blog/leadership-communication.
29. Zeidan, F., S. K. Johnson, B. J. Diamond, and Z. David. "Mindfulness Meditation Improves Emotion Regulation and Reduces Emotional Interference on Cognitive Performance." *Personality and Individual Differences* 49, no. 5 (2010): 395–400.
    https://doi.org/10.1016/j.paid.2010.03.040.

Acknowledgments

To God, I owe all the thanks and praise for giving me the drive, intellect, and tenacity to complete another feat that amplifies His favor. I am forever amazed how You continue to blow my mind with the dreams and visions you place on the inside of me – along with the strength to bring them into fruition.

But as it is written, Eye hath not seen, nor ear heard, neither have entered into the heart of man, the things which God hath prepared for them that love him.

— *1 Corinthians 2:9*

****

As a self-publishing author, the pursuit of excellence is both a privilege and a challenge. The freedom to choose the stories we share with the world is both empowering and daunting. Writing this book was a deliberate and meaningful endeavor—one that represents a significant chapter in my professional and family legacy, a responsibility I hold with great care.

From the start, my focus was the reader—the opportunity to release thoughts bottled up in my mind. My goal was to share the many lessons I've gathered over time, ensuring that no insight remained unspoken. While acknowledging every individual who has contributed to my growth is impossible, I am profoundly grateful to all who have influenced my journey.

I never imagined writing a book on leadership. Many other paths were possible, yet I knew these insights were meant for the next generation of leaders. It is for them that I put these words to paper.

This journey has been transformative—filled with challenges, triumphs, and lessons that will stay with me forever. Every experience, both good and bad, has shaped me, imparting wisdom for which I am deeply grateful. Like many of you, I will continue to make mistakes, but I welcome them as opportunities for growth.

To my mom, your pride in me means the world. Hearing your enthusiasm always makes me smile. I hope this publication continues to affirm God's plan.

To every supervisor, manager, director, vice president, and president I've had the privilege to work with—whether you realized it or not, I was watching. I observed how you led, engaged with those around you, and influenced those in your charge. Your leadership left a lasting impression, and I carry those lessons with me.

A special thank you to the leaders who not only led but invested in me—those who encouraged, challenged, and believed in my potential.

Dr. Jack E. Daniels, III

Dr. Howard J. Spearman

Dr. Brian A. Dixon

Terry Everson

Your insight has been invaluable, and I strive to pay that forward in all that I do. In many ways, this book reflects all that I have learned from you.

About the Author

Keyimani L. Alford, PhD, is a transformational leader, educator, author, entrepreneur, and advocate with over two decades of experience in leadership and training development. Committed to advancing equitable access, enhancing student success, and driving strategic institutional growth, he has led initiatives across higher education, non-profits, and community-based organizations. His work ensures that diverse populations receive the resources and support they need to thrive while equipping leaders with the skills to succeed.

A first-generation college graduate, Dr. Alford holds a PhD in Leadership for Higher Education, a master's in business management, and a bachelor's in social welfare—expertise that enables him to navigate the complexities of organizational leadership. His ability to bridge research-based strategies with real-world application has established him as a respected national leader. He has held key roles in higher education, community development, non-profits, and service industries, consistently driving impactful change.

Dr. Alford is the author of Oakland Hills, Milwaukee Rivers and Keywords Unlocked Motivational Planner, both of which explore themes of resilience, self-discovery, and personal growth. His latest book, Unshaken Leadership: A Practical Blueprint for Overcoming Challenges, Learning from Mistakes, and Growing in Confidence, provides a powerful guide for leaders seeking to navigate adversity with clarity and strength.

Residing in Milwaukee, Wisconsin, he continues to inspire others through his work, sharing vulnerable lessons of perseverance and optimism to create a better world for all that listen.

Connect with him today!

www.drkeyspeaks.com
https://www.facebook.com/drkeyspeaks/
https://www.linkedin.com/in/keyimanialford/

By Leadership Expert & Motivational Speaker

KEYIMANI L. ALFORD, PhD

Now Available on Amazon

Sign up for Dr. Key's newsletter,
The Reflection Corner at www.drkeyspeaks.com

Keywords Unlocked, LLC

www.ingramcontent.com/pod-product-compliance
Lightning Source LLC
Chambersburg PA
CBHW020931090426
42736CB00010B/1107